Streaming ... Heaven's Flow

Companion

Study Guide

by Kent Henry

Abbreviation Legend

AMP - The Amplified Bible
ASV - The American Standard Version
Bas. - The New Testament in Basic English
BER - Berkeley Version of the New Testament
BBE - The Bible in Basic English
CJB - The Complete Jewish Bible
CON - The Epistles of Paul (W.J. Conbeare)
DeW - A Rendering of the Book of Psalms (John DeWitt)
ERV - Easy to Read Version
GLT - Green's Literal Translation
Har. - The Psalms for Today: A New Translation from the Hebrew into Current English (R.K. Harrison)
HCS - Holman Christian Standard Bible
Jerus. - The Jerusalem Bible
KJV - King James Version
KNOX - The Knox Bible
MNT - Mace New Testament
Mof. - A New Translation of the Bible (James Moffatt)
MSG - The Message

NAS - New American Standard
NCV - New Century Version
NEB - The New English Bible
NKJV - New King James Version
NLV - New Life Bible
NLT - New Living Translation
PBV - The Psalms in the Book of Common Prayer of the Anglican Church
Phi. - J.B. Phillips New Testament
REB - The Emphasized Bible
RHE - Douay-Rheims Bible
RSV - Revised Standard Version
Sprl. - A Translation of the Old Testament Scriptures From the Original Hebrew (Helen Spurrell)
TCNT - Twentieth Century New Testament
WEB - World English Bible
WYC - The Wycliffe Bible (1395)
YLT - Young's Literal Translation

Introduction

Over thirty years ago, the Lord gave me this instruction:

"Kent, teach My Body how to intermingle praise with prayer and worship with intercession."

While processing through this word, several thoughts came to my mind. If God's people, who love to worship and love His presence ever learned to combine their worship with intercession, there would be explosive results for the greater glory of God.

The power of our praise joined with strong prayer is part of "Streaming in Heaven's Flow." The dynamics of worship, prayer and music triumph over the powers of darkness. When we join our worship directly to intercession, the plans and purposes of God are made more fully manifest in the earth.

One of my greatest dreams, one of my greatest desires is to see the majority of the American Church praying at a much higher level. I have been ministering on the road for over 30 years. On average, I have done 32 Worship Weekends a year during that time period. I have a fairly good idea of who the American Church is and what the American Church is not. I know for sure that prayerlessness is a major part of what is killing the American Church.

To be very clear, one of our greatest weaknesses is the lack of prayer, intercession, devotion to Jesus and deeper worship in both church leadership and the congregations themselves.

There is a Biblical fix to all of this. Pray more, Worship more. Not in a boring fashion but truly with the Holy Spirit's leadership and touch on it.

This is the time we must grow the devotional life of everyday believers, flowing in deeper worship and greater prayer. This is a high priority in the heart of the Lord. I know that there is exponential power available whenever we merge worship, prayer and music together.

Each chapter will unfold a powerful truth of how to activate yourself and other believers in higher grade prayer and worship. Worship, prayer and music are "Built to Run Together," praise with prayer, worship with intercession. "Jesus is the Core of Everything" and our focus and attention should be daily on the worthy Lamb that was slain.

So we center all that we do around the Bible. Hopefully we are sensing an urgency to get busy with Jesus in the ministry He is currently doing . . . "He ever lives to make intercession (Hebrews 7:25). "

So please enjoy and study diligently this Companion Study Guide. It is time for all of us to start "Streaming in Heaven's Flow." And here is His prayer He told us to pray, "Your Kingdom come and Your will be done" and let it be all over the earth.

This is our time of awakening so let's .... **"Take Heed, Watch and Pray."**

Pressing on in Christ Jesus,
Kent Henry

Streaming in Heaven's Flow - Companion Study Guide

A Prayer Centered Church - Empowering Churchwide Prayer

Section 1 - Table of Contents

Section 2 - Table of Contents

Section 3 - Table of Contents

Appendices

    Psalms for Prayer: Psalm 29, 82, 144
    New Testament Prayers: Ephesians Chapters 1 and 5

Answer Key

Built to Run Together
Passionate Worship and Zealous Prayer

The **Worship, Music** Realm - Anointed Music is a Tool and a Weapon: Isaiah 30:32

The **Prayer** Realm - Pray at all times: Ephesians 6:18

Over thirty years ago, the Lord gave me this instruction:
"Kent, teach My Body how to - intermingle **praise** with **prayer** and
worship with **intercession**."

While processing through this word, several thoughts came to my mind. If God's people, who love to worship and love His presence, ever learned to combine their worship with prayer and intercession there would be explosive results for the greater glory of God.

1. Intermingle Praise with Prayer and Worship with Intercession

Focused prayer riding on top of the zeal of worship is unstoppable.

This is why we emulate (strive to equal) Heaven's model of the elders in worship using harps representing music and worship in one hand and golden bowls in the other which are full of incense. This incense is our prayers definitively called the "prayers of the saints."

A. Our Prayers and Worship Rise as Incense before the Lord.

> **Revelation 5:8** - "*When He had taken the scroll, the four living creatures and the twenty-four elders fell down before the Lamb,*
>
> *each one holding a* **harp** *and golden* **bowls** **full of incense**, *which are the* **prayers of the saints**."

What was it that the Lord wanted of His People and for His House all along?

B. This is What Jesus said, `**My House Shall Be Called A House of Prayer.**'

> **Matthew 21:12 - 13**
>
> [12] *And Jesus entered the temple and drove out all those who were buying and selling in the temple, and overturned the tables of the money changers and the seats of those who were selling doves.*
> [13] *He said to them, "It is written, `MY HOUSE SHALL BE CALLED A HOUSE OF PRAYER'; but you are making it a ROBBERS' DEN." (made it a den of plunderers.)* (GLT)
>
> *My house was* **designated** *a house of prayer; You have made it a hangout for thieves.* (MSG)

 Revelations and Thoughts: _____

2. The Power of the Worship Realm and the Music Realm

While in the worship realm, **all the borders are gone** and the enemy is forbidden from stopping your heart and your voice from yielding its full praise and worship.

A. Anointed Music, a Tool and a Weapon

> **Isaiah 30:32 -** *And every blow of the rod of punishment, which the LORD will lay on him (King of Assyria), will be* ***with the music*** *of (Israel's) tambourines and lyres; when in battle He attacks (Assyria), brandishing weapons, He will fight them.* (NAS, AMP)
>
> *. . . He will beat them* ***to the music*** *of tambourines and harps;*
> *He will fight against them with His mighty weapons.* (NCV)

B. Praying and Singing Breaks Chains: Supernatural Results Follow

> **Acts 16:25 - 26**
> [25] *But about midnight Paul and Silas were praying and singing hymns of praise to God, and the prisoners were listening to them;*
> [26] *and suddenly there came a great earthquake, so that the foundations of the prison house were shaken; and immediately all the doors were opened and everyone's chains were unfastened. We are living sacrifices, our spiritual service of worship, diligent worship and prayer rises as incense.*

 Revelations and Thoughts: _____

_____

_____

3. The Power of the Prayer Realm

> **Ephesians 6:18 -** *With all prayer and petition* ***pray*** *at* ***all times in the Spirit****, and with this in view, be on the alert with all perseverance and petition for all the saints.*
>
> ***Pray at all times*** *(on every occasion, in every season) in the Spirit, with all [manner of] prayer and entreaty. To that end keep alert and watch with strong purpose and perseverance,* ***interceding*** *in behalf of all the saints (God's consecrated people).* (AMP)

Pray More, Worship More

When you begin to see the **power of corporate prayer, worship, and music** as God created them, you never want to stop doing any of the three.

Many things happen: to and through a person during times of intimate worship and prayer.

A. Greater Light and Revelation . . . floods into and over us as we invest more time in His presence before the throne of God. As a result, our level of discernment is also heightened and we use it more.

B. We are Stronger in Our Ability . . . to get in the flow of intimate worship and prayer because of the extended times of being in His presence. We end up like toned athletes or runners that can go a long time before becoming weary.

C. Hearts Pure, Minds Focused . . . The power of pure worship used at the highest level is like the Refiners Fire that keeps our hearts pure and our minds focused on the Lord.

D. The Knowledge of Who God is . . . and what He does has become more deeply set in our hearts. As we have been faithful to do extended times in the Prayer Room, our eyes and hearts have been opened to some of the deeper things of the Word of God and His ways. The sense of unity and one accord is much stronger.

Revelations and Thoughts: _____

_____

_____

Study, Discuss, Think About:

Grace, justice and faith are released as we pray the Word.

❖ Why is intermingling praise with prayer and worship with intercession important first to the Lord and second to us?

❖ What makes a church a house of prayer and worship instead of just a gathering place for friends?   Why is there joy in the house of prayer?

❖ Many things happen to and through a person during times of intimate worship and prayer. Name two of the four things listed in this teaching that happen to us when we are part of deeper worship and passionate prayer.

Jesus Is The Core of Everything
Dwell, Gaze and Inquire

Three Anchor Points . . . to **dwell** (in His Presence),

to **gaze** (at His Beauty) and

to **inquire** (in His Temple)

Everyone studies these, deeply intaking these truths, living these three things.

1. One Thing - (in three parts)

The basis for everything we do and try to accomplish is stated in Psalm 27. This Psalm reveals David's desire to be in the presence of the Lord. It is a great pattern to follow.

All we do is centered around the Lord, His Presence and His Person, knowing the great worth of the Lord. It's the spirit of seeking, dwelling, gazing, and inquiring.

Psalm 27:4 - *One thing I have asked from the LORD, that I shall* **seek**: *that I may*

a. ***dwell*** *in the house of the LORD all the days of my life, [in His presence] to*

b. ***gaze*** *upon the beauty of the LORD, [to behold His loveliness] and to*

c. ***inquire*** *in His temple [to meditate, consider and study in His temple]*

2. Worthy is the Lamb that was Slain,
He Made Us to Be a Kingdom of Priests

Revelation 5:6, 9 - 10

[6] *And I saw in the middle of the throne and of the four living creatures and in the midst of the elders, stood a Lamb as it had been slain . . .* (NAS, KJV)

[9] *And they (the four living creatures and the twenty-four elders) sang a* **new song**, *saying,*
"Worthy are You to take the scroll and to break its seals;
for You were slain, and purchased for God **with Your blood** *men from every tribe and tongue and people and nation."*

[10] *"You have made them to be a* **kingdom** *and* **priests to our God**; *and they will reign upon the earth."*

What they declared in the New Song

1. Worthy . . . because He was slain, gave His life for the redemption of all men
2. Worthy . . . because He purchased with His blood, human beings
3. Worthy . . . because He assembled all of the redeemed into a massive Priesthood

This Jesus is beautiful beyond all description. He is stunning. He is glorious. He is overwhelming. This is why **Jesus has to be the core** of everything that we are doing and that we are all about.

 Revelations and Thoughts: _____

_____

3. Who is it That Heaven Sees? Revelation 5:6, 9 - 10

A. The Person of the Lord Jesus - Jesus was a real person who walked on the earth. The very being of the Son of God was here in human form and then returned to all of His glory. He is currently seen in Heaven in all of His awesomeness and all of His beauty but now with a glorified body that has scars on it.

1. Jesus, the Lamb of God, slain   2. He is beautiful beyond all description
    3. Heaven sees Him "ever living to make intercession"

B. Beholding Who Jesus Is - It will take dedicated, additional amounts of time to even scratch the surface to know the full revelation of Jesus.

C. You Are Worthy of It All

> **Revelation 4:11** - *Thou art **worthy**, O Lord, to receive glory and honor and power: for Thou hast created **all** things*   (KJV)

1. All the saints and angels bow
2. Elders cast their crowns
3. Four living creatures cry "holy" continually

4. What Heaven Knows

A. The Description of Who He is

1. **His head** and His hair were like white wool, like snow

2. **His eyes** were like a flame of fire

3. **His feet** were like burnished bronze, glowing in a furnace

4. **His voice** was like the sound of many waters

5. Out of **His mouth** came a sharp two-edged sword

6. **His face** was like the sun shining in its strength

B. From a Lamb to a Lion, Jesus is Coming Back Again!

All of Heaven recognizes the "power of the life of the crucified Lamb." When you add the power of His blood and the power of His Cross as a legal instrument, you are beginning to understand what Jesus looks like to them in Heaven.

5. How Then Does Heaven Respond?   The "Greatness and the Glory"

Worship Full of Reverential Awe . . . . Jesus is:

> . . . the Master Lord over all spirits.
> . . . His light and power dispels all darkness.
> . . . His great grace is superior to the works of men.
> . . . His justice triumphs over all wickedness.
> . . . And His redemption covers the fallen state of man.

Again:

1. All the saints and angels bow   2. Elders cast their crowns
3. Four living creatures cry "holy" continually

6. Lifestyle - Living before the Lord as a Royal Priesthood

> **Psalm 16:8 -** *I have **set** the LORD **continually before** me;*
> *because He is at my right hand, I will not be shaken.*
>
> *I have set the LORD **always** before me;* (NKJV)
> *I **keep** the LORD (ADONAI) before me always.* (NCV)
>
> *I set the Lord always in my sight.* (RHE) *I keep the Lord in mind always.* (HCS)

I find this one of the most important aspects of living a godly and close to God life. In my own walk with the Lord, I naturally received Jesus as my friend and understood that He would be ever present with me.

So I set the Lord continually before me and He's always in my heart and mind. This way I am always ready to minister, to worship, to pray and be a blessing.

7. Jesus' Servanthood and Humility

If you want to be great, become the servant of all. **Humble yourself** . . .
It is the choice of your heart and will.

A. Three "M's" - The Necessary Parts for Equipping Others

Model the truth,   **mentor** the ways of the Lord,   and gifts and talents are **multiplied**.

> **Matthew 11:29 -** *(Jesus speaking) Take My yoke upon you, and learn of Me;*
> *for I am meek and lowly of heart; you shall find rest unto your souls.*
> *[I am gentle and humble of heart.]* (KJV, AMP)

People are watching you. You are an example or a model even if you don't realize it. So use your life and be a mentor. Teach people by living a lifestyle pleasing to the Lord. In doing so, you will multiply the gifts and talents God has invested in you and others.

B. Clothe Yourselves with Humility

I Peter 5:5 - *and all of you, clothe yourselves with **humility** toward one another,*
for GOD IS OPPOSED TO THE PROUD, BUT GIVES GRACE TO THE HUMBLE.
***Clothe** (apron) **yourselves**, all of you, with humility*
[as the garb of a servant, so that its covering cannot possibly be stripped from you,
with freedom from pride and arrogance] toward one another.

[He opposes, frustrates, and defeats them],
***but gives grace** (favor, blessing) **to the humble**. (AMP)*

This scripture is so telling of the desire of the heart of the Father. Humble, humility, lowly and meek. In God's plan, He knew humility would be **attractive to every generation.**

So humility and being humble is possibly one of God's all time principles on how we should walk in this life and the true power release that comes because of it. It is time to break out our Bibles, and do a current Bible study on humility, humble, meekness and lowly of heart.

Revelations and Thoughts: _____

_____

_____

Study, Discuss, Think About:

❖ What are the three things David asked of the Lord in Psalm 27:4? (fill in the blank)

D _____   G _____   I _____

In the House of the Lord   Upon the beauty   in His Temple

❖ Who is it Heaven sees and how do they respond? Revelation 5: 6, 9 - 10

❖ What are the three M's and what purpose do they serve?
On a scale of 1 - 10 with 10 being the highest, how important is humility to Jesus?

The Prayers of the Saints
Incense Is Rising

1. Golden Bowls Full of Incense - which are the prayers of the saints

Revelation 5:7 - 8

[7] *And He came [a Lamb standing, as if slain] and*
took the book out of the right hand of Him who sat on the throne.

[8] *When He had taken the book [the scroll] ; the four living creatures and*
the twenty-four elders fell down before the Lamb,
*each one **holding a harp** and golden bowls **full of incense,***

which are **(a)** *the **prayers of the saints** [holy ones].*

*Each was holding a harp (lute or guitar), and they had golden bowls **full of incense***
(fragrant spices and gums for burning), which are the
(b) ***prayers** of **God's people** (the saints).* (AMP) *. . .*
the prayers of Christ's people. (TCNT)

. . . pots made of gold, full of special perfume, filled with pieces of incense, (CJB)
which are the prayers of the **(c)** **people who belong to God.** (NLV)

*. . . [they] went down on their faces before the Lamb, having every one an **instrument of music***
*and gold vessels full of **perfumes**, which are the prayers of the saints.* (BBE)

A. The Prayers of the People Who Belong to God (Covenant Rights)

We are Christ's people, **covenant-rights** people praying in the name of Jesus, by His precious blood. We stand in the power of the life of the crucified Lamb as intercessors.

B. The Prayers of the Saints: intercessions, petitioning the Lord

Prayer - to ask with earnest or zeal, to entreat, [to supplicate: petition and implore]
in worship: to address our Supreme Being with reverence and adoration, then
to pour words out like water as in violent rain. (Noah Webster)

Revelation 8:3- 4

[3] *Another angel came and stood at the altar, holding a golden censer;*
and much incense was given to him, so that he might add it (give it) to the
***prayers of all the saints** [holy ones] on the golden altar which was before the throne.*

[4] *the smoke of the **incense**, with the **prayers** of the **saints**,*
went up before God out of the angel's hand.

 Revelations and Thoughts: _____

_____

2. The Prayer of the Upright is His Delight

> **Proverbs 15:8**
>
> *The sacrifice of the wicked is an abomination to the LORD,
> but the **prayer** of the upright is **His delight**.*
>
> *ADONAI detests the sacrifices of the wicked but **delights** in the prayers of the upright.* (CJB)
>
> *GOD can't stand pious poses, He delights in **genuine** prayers, of the faithful is **His joy**.* (MSG, NLV)

A. How We Spend Our Words? The power of words, to pray and to bless

Walk in a lifestyle that speaks words of encouragement and knows how to flow in prayers of blessing. The power of our words lift off things that are negative like words that have brought hurt or harm. Our words have healing in them. They have restorative power.

3. Prayers as Incense
[An Evening Prayer for Sanctification and Protection. David's Psalm]

> **Psalm 141:2** - *May **my prayer** be counted **[fixed]** as incense before You;
> the lifting up of my hands as the evening offering.*
>
> *May my prayer be like **special perfume** before You...given on the **altar** in **worship**.* (NLV)

A. David Loved Prayer, he begs of God that his prayers might be heard and answered, that the Lord would be well pleased with him in it, well pleased with his *praying* and the *lifting up of his hands in prayer.*

Prayer to David denotes both the elevation and enlargement of **his desire** and
the out-goings of his **hope** and **expectation.**

B. The Lifting Up of the Hands signifying the lifting up of the heart, is being used instead of lifting up the sacrifices which were heaved and waved before the Lord.

Prayer is a spiritual sacrifice; it is the offering up of the soul, and its **best affections**, to God.

C. He Prays that this may be set forth and directed before God *as the incense* which was daily burned upon the golden altar. And *as the evening sacrifice,* (perhaps) with an eye to Christ, who, in the evening of the world and in the evening of the day, was to offer up Himself a sacrifice of atonement.

Note: Prayer is a sweet-smelling savor to God, as incense, which yet has no savor
without **fire;** nor has prayer without the fire of holy love and fervor.

Revelations and Thoughts: _____

_____

_____

4. Worship and Intercession ... are ... Harp and Bowl Ministry

Revelation 5:8

[They] went down on their faces before the Lamb, (fell down and worshipped the Lamb)

*having every one an **instrument of music**, and*
*gold vessels full of **perfumes**, which are the prayers of the saints.* (BBE, MSG)

A. The Power of Anointed Music

played through consecrated vessels has its own **authority**.

The Lord created music that flows with power on it for a reason. And that reason is music has the power to transport: it has the ability to carry people to a different place. Music has lifting power in it.

B. As Anointed Music Flows,

it helps maintain our concentration, our focus and attention for effective prayer.

Music helps focus the attention of those doing prayer and intercession on the Lord. It helps maintain our concentration for effective prayer.

Music (harping) also becomes a weapon of war in the spirit realm, just as God has always intended it. The Lord knew that worship and intercession or harp and bowl ministry would work well together and it would have power over the kingdom of darkness.

C. The Prayers of the Saints: perfumed incense that rises before the Lord

Singing and Praying the Word of God: our prayers fill the golden bowls.

God shapes the world by prayer. Prayers are deathless.
They outlive the lives of those who uttered them. (E.M. Bounds)

Singing and praying the Word releases the help of the Lord for the afflicted and downtrodden and releases the power and judgments of God against His enemies.

Revelations and Thoughts: _____

_____

Study, Discuss, Think About:

❖ As the Elders worshipped the Lamb of God, in Revelation 5, what were they holding in their hands? Why are these elements important to us today?

❖ Why did David love prayer? And why was it important to him?

❖ The power of anointed music through consecrated vessels has its own aut_____.

As anointed music flows, it helps maintain our con_____ and fo_____.

This is How We Do Corporate Prayer and Worship

Some of Our Story

At Destiny Church, in St. Louis, our Prayer Room has been up and running for several years. We started with twelve hours a week
　　　　　Monday - Thursday, three hours a day (9 am to 12 pm), in January of 2008.

We had "fits and starts" at the beginning and had to learn about . . .
consistency, stamina, and **perseverance** in worship and with prayer. Like most other believers, we were focused on pulling off great weekend services to keep everybody excited and plugged in.

The weekend service model was all that we had seen and that system had little need for a greater spiritual lifestyle, a lifestyle which includes diligent prayer and seeking the Lord. That all began to change as we pressed in to know how and more about a deeper prayer life.

We are currently praying all day on Tuesdays, starting at 9:00 am and going until 8:30 pm. It is almost twelve hours in one day. With additional hours on other days, we have averaged 24 hours a week since 2008.

1. Different Types of Prayer Room Sets

Devotional Sets: This is time of deeper worship, where we linger and wait before the Lord. This is a great time to open the Bible and mediate on His Word. It is important to go slow and ponder a few verses at a time.

Adoration Sets: This is where a prayer leader begins to adore the Lord praying and speaking out the attributes and great qualities of the Lord. The singers still sing, it is more in line with tenderly adoring the Lord.

Worship with the Word Sets: The chorus leader and singers start this set by singing the Word of God first. Then a prayer leader begins to slowly read and pray prayers around the Word. Psalms work great for this type of set.

Intercession Sets: This seems to be the most intense type of set. The prayer leader actually starts this set off with praying the Word and the singers sing off of what he or she is praying. We run our sets with full bands where the music, the energy and dynamic range is flowing and changing.

2. Ninety Minute Prayer Room Sets

We run ninety minute prayer room sets (an hour and a half).
Each set consists of:　　(2) two 20 minute worship segments and
　　　　　　　　　　　　　(2) two 20 minute Prayer Room cycles.

The worship team is playing the full ninety minutes, while four different Prayer Leaders each pray ten minutes at a time. Here's an example of a typical "Evening Intercession Set:"

a. 7:00 pm to 7:20 pm - 20 minutes of deeper worship, pressing into the Lord

This is devotional in nature, directly to the Lord and includes times of adoration toward Him. It is mostly worship based, not praise based. These are songs and singing that are directly to the Lord, not about Him.　　[Vertical worship versus horizontal praise.]

b. 7:20 pm to 7:40 pm - 20 minutes of directed prayer and intercession (A Prayer Room Cycle)

[A Prayer Room cycle - is built on set topics or themes you decide ahead of time]

Examples: Human sex trade trafficking, prayer for Israel's Salvation, praying the Apostolic prayers from Ephesians, Philippians, and Colossians (found in Chapter One of each book)

c. 7:40 pm to 8:00 pm - Back to 20 minutes of worship: (or so . . .)

We start refocusing on the greatness of our God, His goodness and the facts of who He is and what He does. We are using songs that have lyrics that lend themselves to more of a glorious worship, speaking of His attributes and nature.

d. 8:00 pm to 8:20 pm - 20 minutes of directed prayer and intercession - (A Prayer Room Cycle)

The cool thing about the times listed here is they are always in flux . . . they are not so rigid that we can't follow the Holy Spirit or flow with something that gets the "burn" on it, something that catches fire, we can run with that for minutes on end.

Revelations and Thoughts: _____

_____

3. Musical Foundation

A guitar/piano player starts a chord progression that creates a **music bed**. It is a music foundation for singing or praying the Word of God. This music is usually not too busy or too aggressive, but carefully supports what a singer or prayer leader is doing.

It is God's desire to flow with us and through us for the river flow that helps passionate worship and greater intercession.

As a prayer time continues, the music grows in terms of dynamic range or in complexity to help give force to what is being sung or played. I have found that the chord progression can flow and be strong for minutes on end. It's the musicians' responsibility to be sensitive to the dynamics of the situation and change the music to "grow" with the prayer time.

A. Providing Time and Space for Prayer Leading

The music bed provides a space for prayer leading as well as singers making up spontaneous lines or choruses to what is being prayed. There is a powerful interaction between a prayer leader and the assigned singers that is interfaced to the on going music.

The prayer leader may pray for three to four minutes using a Psalm or a New Testament apostolic prayer. Then the singers will pick up a sentence or a few of the words that have just been prayed. They fit these words to a melody that flows with the chord progression that the musicians are playing. This lasts for the fifteen minute prayer cycle until we are finished.

B. The Power of Resounding Music unto the Lord - Psalm 92:1 - 3

[1] *It is good to give thanks to the LORD and to sing praises to Your name, O Most High;*

[2] *To declare Your loving kindness **in the morning** and Your faithfulness **by night**,*

[3] *With the ten-stringed lute and with the harp, with **resounding music** upon the lyre on the ten strings, and on the harp; on the lyre **with sounding music**.* (GLT) ***accompanied by** the harp and lute, the **harmony** of the lyre, (with) the **full-bodied music** of strings.* (NLT, MSG)

*God, it is good to **play music for you** on ten-stringed instruments, harps, and lyres.* (ERV)

4. The Prayer Room is about Development

We learned in our first year of the **Prayer Room,** it is **about development** of people's gifts, talents and their hearts. Even though we are focusing on the Lord, worship and intercession, we really pay attention to growing people spiritually.

This is a great place for younger people and home schooler's to begin their development. We give them the same music charts we are doing for the Prayer Room Set and they play or sing along. This gives them a chance to learn and make mistakes without the added pressure of "being up front."

A. The "Must - Do's:" For A Prayer Room to Work These Things Must be Established

❖ **Vision**: Write it down and make it plain (don't assume people already know it)

❖ **Direction**: Be very definite and clear about where you are going

❖ **Organization**: Be sure to utilize the people whose temperament and skill set is available

❖ **Values**: Believing in the same things together is super important
  ▪ (Why a Prayer Room? Importance of prayer?
  ▪ Doing the ministry that Jesus does - intercession)

❖ **Commitment and Consistency**: This takes true commitment of mind and heart. Sign up for times that are doable for you and be diligent week after week.

Revelations and Thoughts: _____

_____

B. Gathering and Activating

Find and invite people to join in and join up. All hands on deck!
Everybody gets involved either playing and singing or prayer leading.
Spending and investing this time will activate people's gifts and callings.

1. Everyone is on the lookout: who can join up and become a part of the Prayer Room.

2. Everyone is all about **"activating"** the gifts, talents and anointing
of new singers, musicians, prayer leaders and media - tech help.

Super Important Note:

Teenagers and Tweeners (9 - 12 year olds) really take to the Prayer Room
environment. They love music, enjoy worship and pray with simplicity and
passion. It's fresh and powerful because they haven't been talked out of it yet.
So don't leave them out!

Revelations and Thoughts: _____

_____

_____

This is Why We Do Corporate Prayer and Worship

1. Join in with the Ministry Jesus is Currently Doing

The fulfilling our priestly calling is to do the ministry of worship and prayer; all believers can be involved in the ministry that Jesus Himself is doing.

> **Hebrews 7:25**   He (Jesus) always lives to **make intercession**
>
> *Therefore He is able also to save forever (save completely) those who draw near to God through Him, since He Jesus) always lives to **make intercession** for them.*
>
> *Since He (Jesus) is always living to make petition to God (the Father) and **intercede** with Him and **intervene** for them (His believers).* (AMP)

What kind of high honor is this that we can learn how to pray and intercede like Jesus does? We are co-laborers with Him in this powerful ministry that brings Heaven down to earth and opens gateways to blessing.

Stop for a minute and mediate on this fact: He intercedes for you right now as part of His body and His beloved ones. This Jesus kind of intercession moves the heart of our Heavenly Father and changes things on the earth.

One of the greatest reasons we're on the earth is to be **active** as **worshipping intercessors**. There is a greater empowerment when worship and prayer are mixed together! We are fulfilling our **eternal destiny** as lovers of Jesus and the Royal Priesthood.

2. Jesus Told Us: Pray "the Lord of the Harvest" to Send Out Laborers

> **Luke 10:2**
>
> *Then He said to them, "The harvest truly is great, but the laborers are few;*
> *therefore **pray to the Lord of the harvest** to send out laborers into His harvest.* (NKJV)
>
> *He said to them, "There are a great many people to harvest, but there are only a few workers.*
> *So **pray to God, Who owns the harvest,***
> *that He will send more workers to help gather His harvest.* (NCV)
>
> **Matthew 9:38**
>
> *Therefore (you) pray the Lord of the harvest to send out laborers into **His harvest**."* (NKJV, KJV)

A. Prayer is Necessary on the Earth because it is Vital for the Harvest

From the scripture above, Jesus told us prophetically ahead of time, as a matter of fact, that prayer affects the intake of the harvest. So every believer in every church should systematically pray this prayer but do it supported by deep worship and anointed music.

B. This is What We Know for Sure from Jesus' Words . . .

1. The harvest is great and abundant. The great harvest is yet to come!

Diligent prayer does affect the amount of the harvest and the timing of when it starts and how long it can run.

C. What We Know for Sure

is that there are not enough laborers, the laborers are yet too few.

Our prayers rise as incense before God Almighty and they are stored in golden bowls. So our prayers have bearing on a greater number of laborers (missionaries, market place believers and evangelism) coming forth.

3. Pray This Way and Pray It Every Day

Matthew 6:9 - 15

[9] *"Pray, then, in this way: `Our Father who is in heaven, Hallowed be Your name.*
[10] *Your kingdom come. Your will be done, on earth as it is in heaven.*
[11] *Give us this day our daily bread.*
[12] *And forgive us our debts, as we also have forgiven our debtors.*
[13] *And do not lead us into temptation, but deliver us from evil.*
For Yours is the kingdom and the power and the glory forever. Amen.'
[14] *For if you forgive others for their transgressions,*
your heavenly Father will also forgive you.
[15] *But if you do not forgive others, then your Father will not forgive your transgressions."*

A. Why We Pray is Internalized in
The Seven Aspects of the "Our Father" Prayer

1. Jesus declares in this prayer that God is our Father and He reigns from Heaven.

2. His name is holy and as a result, has power to affect change on the earth.

3. God's Kingdom is real and it actually exists. Our cry continually then is to be "Your Kingdom come, Your Will be Done." With faith in our hearts we pray it.

4. Jesus revealed His own desire and a super important theological point, God desires that what is going on in Heaven would be found on earth in the same way.

5. We all have a need for daily bread. So it is our prayer on a daily basis. It is God's desire to give and He made it a part of His promise and provision - daily bread.

6. The power to forgive is our choice. Nobody really wins when we walk in unforgiveness.

7. Be aware of the temptations that are around us every day. This is such a great prayer because it ends with deliver us from evil.

In light of these elements within the Our Father, there is a simple pattern that can be followed and prayed over a long period of time. God is our Father and His name is holy.

The Kingdom is real and the Lord wants to see Heaven on Earth. A cool prayer of humility is give us the day, our daily bread. Forgiveness brings freedom. He gave us the power to resist and overcome temptation.

4. Jesus Gave Us an Advocate, A Helper, His Name is Holy Spirit

Growing up as a little boy or girl, it's a normal desire to ask for help. It's because of pride and stubbornness that we refuse to be open and ask for help. Romans 8 tells us exactly what we can do now. When we do not know how to pray, the Holy Spirit Himself intercedes for us.

Romans 8:26

*In the same way the Spirit also helps our weakness; for we do not know how to **pray** as we should, but the Spirit Himself intercedes for us with groanings too deep for words.*

Relying on the Person and the power of the Holy Spirit is a life-long adventure. So let us pray and understand these three distinct points:

A. How glad are we that the Holy Spirit helps our weaknesses?

B. We do not always know how to pray and that's okay because the Holy Spirit has already searched the Father's heart.

C. The Holy Spirit Himself intercedes for us with groanings too deep for words.

5. Desperate Prayer Riding on a Wave Worship

The power of worship releases His presence,   [our **entry point**].
Desperate prayer ascending into Heaven,   [opens **spiritual gateways**].
The depth of worship flows with spiritual might on it,   [a **tool** and **weapon** of priesthood].
The heart of intercession has real fire and passion,   [blessing people, breaking the darkness].

Every believer is called do some form of worship and prayer,

- add heart-felt prayers to your worship . . .
- add the understanding of God's justice to your prayers . . .
- add persistent intercession to God's justice . . .
- add worship back in, and start all over again.

 Revelations and Thoughts: _____

_____

Study, Discuss, Think About: Jesus does the ministry of intercession.

- What is the ministry Jesus is currently doing and how do we become part of that?

- In Luke 10:2, there are three major points marked A, B and C. Reread the three points and write down which one seems the most important to you at this time of your life.

- Name 3 of the 7 aspects of the "Our Father." List them in order of significance to you.

Psalms, Hymns and Spiritual Songs: Speak to One Another

1. Holy Songs of Praise and Songs of the Holy Spirit
Training Singers and Musicians to Flow

Ephesians 5:19 - *But drink deeply of God's Spirit.* **Speak out to one another** *in*

> *(1) psalms and (2) hymns and (3) spiritual songs, offering praise with voices [and instruments] and making melody with all your heart to the Lord,*

> *Joining with one another in* **holy songs** *of praise and* **of the Spirit,**
> *using your voice in songs and making melody in your heart to the Lord;* (BBE)

> *. . . singing, and* **striking the strings**, *with your heart unto the Lord;* (REB)

A. Learning the Bible by Singing Scripture Choruses

In the 1970's and 80's, we learned the Bible by singing Scripture choruses. There is probably no other way we would have known so much of the Bible without the power of singing the Word of God. Thousands of people from non-Bible reading backgrounds came into the greater depths of the Word because the Word was put (set) to music.

B. A Necessary Spiritual Skill - Singing the Word

In the same way, we are entering into a time where singing and praying the Word will be a necessary skill to sustain a deeper walk with the Lord and get through the harder times of real life. Most churches and prayer groups have never really learned to sing and pray the Word of God at a high level. This is the time to train and begin "doing it."

Revelations and Thoughts: _____

_____

_____

2. Flowing in the Songs of the Holy Spirit

Colossians 3:16 - Songs of David - Songs of Heaven

> *Let the* **word of Christ** *(our Lord) richly dwell within you, with all wisdom teaching and admonishing one another with*
> ***psalms, hymns*** *and* **spiritual songs**, *singing with thankfulness in your hearts to God.*

> *Sing the* **Songs of David** *and the* **church songs**
> *and the* **songs of Heaven** *with hearts full of thanks to God.* (NLV)

A. Psalm - Sing the Songs of David. There are 150 Psalms available for singing and praying. We are not only to quicken and encourage ourselves, but teach and admonish one another.   ("The Treasury of David" by Charles Spurgeon)

B. Hymn - a song, an ode or a poem in honor of God put to music.
Keep singing the church (Gospel) songs.

C. Spiritual Songs - songs of the moment, spontaneous songs, and the songs of Heaven
These are **songs generated from the hearts** of believers touched by the power of the Holy Spirit.

3. Prophetic Worship: Bubble Up from the Inside

prophesy - naba' - [nä·vä'] - to prophesy under influence of divine spirit

to cause to **bubble up** . . . (fountains, gurgling streams);
to **pour forth** words abundantly as it done by those who speak or [sing] with passion or divine emotion of mind or heart

This definition of the prophetic is simple to do and understand. The Lord intended that every believer would speak by inspiration of their own heart. They would live under the divine inspiration of the Holy Spirit. It applies to our everyday life and all that we do in it.

prophesy - nabiy' - [nä·vē'] - those actuated (moved to action) by the divine Spirit.
spokesman, speaker, prophet: prophecy, them that prophesy.

4. Putting the Word of God to Melody and Song

A. Releasing the Power While Using the Word of God

As your church singers and musicians learn how to do this, three powerful things begin to happen: They are . . .

1. Releasing the power of God's Word in a consistent and long-term manner.
2. Using the Word of God to bind up principalities/powers in the kingdom of darkness.
3. Learning, memorizing and getting the Scripture deep in their hearts.

The Scriptures are being sung in our churches and our modern choruses are a large part of our time in the Prayer Room. We are so much stronger spiritually because we are singing and praying the Word of God.

Words that we sing and put to music will be remembered longer and inscribed deeper into our hearts and minds. The nature of singing and music causes this to happen.

Psalm 119: 170 - 172

[170] *Let my supplication come before You; deliver me according to Your word.*
[171] *Let my lips utter praise, for You teach me Your statutes.*
[172] *Let my tongue sing of Your Word, for all Your commandments are righteousness.*

 Revelations and Thoughts: _____

5. I Will Sing of Your Word

Sing - [`anah]- to sing, utter tunefully, melodious: having a pleasant melody

A. God's People Singing and Praying the Bible

It is through the living, enduring Word of God that we have all that we have anyway. Jesus upholds all things by the word of His power. It just makes sense that we would invest time in singing and praying it.

B. When "Word of God" Seeds are Planted

they will always germinate because they are full of the Life of God. Intercession and prayer combined with anointed music should be flowing in every section of the earth.

This imperishable seed is the Word of God that brings great results. The hidden treasure of the Bible is the reason that singing and praying the Word is counted as a necessary stream of any Prayer Room or prayer movement.

C. Anything Spoken Can be Sung

uttered tunefully, sung to spontaneous, pleasant melodies, melodies arising from the heart.

God's Word prayed out loud . . . while singers echo His Word in song . . . supported by anointed music and worship is an unstoppable force in **activating the Word** that cannot return void.

6. Praying the Bible is a Powerful Force

for the greater release of His Word, with His light and power on it, as it streams mercy, grace and justice and faith.

Romans 10:17 - *Faith comes by **hearing**, and **hearing** by the Word of God.*

A. Singing and Praying the Word in Power

[The five major areas for Biblical praying]

1. Apostolic prayers of the New Testament
   (Prayers from the heart of God's Apostles and Overseers)

2. Worship Hymns from the Book of Psalms
   (Songs declaring the worth and attributes of the Lord)

3. Prayers from the Book of Psalms
   (Songs of prayer from the Psalmists heart, i.e. David, Asaph)

4. Song of Solomon - The Love Song of the Ravished Heart
   (The story of the interplay between the bride and the bridegroom)

5. Scriptural theophanies - (God revealing Himself to human beings)

Revelations and Thoughts: _____

_____

_____

7. The Word of God is Living, Active, and Full of Power

A. The Heart and Ability of God's Word

The Word of God is alive and active, it is sharper than a two-edged sword. Think of the innate ability of the Word of God to bring change to a situation or even to an atmosphere when it is sung and prayed out loud over powerfully anointed music.

> **Isaiah 55:11**
>
> *So will **My Word** be which goes forth from My mouth; It will not return to Me **empty** (void or unfulfilled), without accomplishing what I desire, what I **intend**, and without succeeding in the matter for which I sent it.*

B. The Word of God is Piercing.

It is for blessing and binding in prayer and intercession. We must not under value it, and learn the "every-day-ness" of using it in prayer and worship.

 Revelations and Thoughts: _____

_____

Study, Discuss, Think About:

❖ It's all about language. I must include the importance of words of encouragement. Ephesians 5 and Colossians 3 tell us almost exactly the same thing. Let the word of Christ richly dwell within you, speak to one another in Ps_____, hy_____ and spiritual _____.

❖ Concerning prophetic worship and prophetic singing, there is a simple definition found in the Hebrew language. The word is naba' - [nä·vä'] which means to sing or speak under the influence of the Divine Spirit. What is the simple five word definition?
(Hint: It's what fountains and gurgling springs do.)

❖ List three of the five categories of Scriptures listed above that are used for Biblical praying.

Section

Two

Lessons 7 - 12 on intermingling praise with prayer and worship with intercession

Because of Love
Love . . . Intimacy . . . Encountering God

We Love Him because He First Loved Us.

The reason that we worship is because of Love.

The reason that we pray is because of Love.

. . . sustaining a lifestyle of worship and prayer is fed from the baseline of true love.

> **Jeremiah 31: 3 -** *The LORD appeared to him (Jeremiah) from afar, saying, "I have loved you with an **everlasting love**; therefore I have drawn you with lovingkindness."*
>
> *(The Lord says,) "I love you people with a love that continues **forever**. That is why I have continued **showing you** kindness."* (ERV)

1. Lovers Will Always Outwork Workers

I heard this statement many years ago, "Lovers will always outwork workers because the motivation of their heart is love and not money. Workers rarely outwork lovers."

I want you to pray at the highest levels. I want you to do worship and intercession that really brings change. But you must first ask the Lord for the genuine revelation of the magnitude of His love toward you.

I use the word magnitude because it is in line with science on star magnitudes. The understanding of a stars brightness or mass is simply overwhelming. When you compare a light bulb in the lamp in your living room to the brightness of the noon day sun, it is hard to grasp because of the huge difference between the two.

Thank God that the revelation of His love is portioned out little by little helping us understand the **gravity of His love**. His drawing power, His ability to cover you along with the great plan and destiny is now unfolding in your life.

2. It Is Because of Love

> **Jeremiah 31: 3** - *From a distance ADONAI appeared to me, [saying,]*
> *"I love you with an everlasting love; this is why **in My grace** I draw you to Me."* (CJB)

It is because of love. Love is the true motivation of why we get married; why we have best friends; why we have babies; why people care for strangers, orphans and widows; why we cry at the loss of a loved one. Love is the **true motivator** as we learn how to sit and adore the Lord. Love helps us learn how to sit quietly and meditate on the Word of God. The call **to work** in prayer and intercession has to be preceded by our love for God and for people.

This is our starting line. This is our baseline. We don't pray and do worship because we are workers, we do these things because of the unfolding revelation of the power of knowing

God intimately. The communion of the Holy Spirit has much to do with intimacy. All things were created for His pleasure.

 Revelations and Thoughts: _____

3. Learning the Deeper Realm of Intimacy

> **John 1:18** - *No man has ever seen God at any time; the only unique Son . . .*
> *Who is in the bosom [in the **intimate** presence] of the Father . . .* (AMP)

Intimacy is the true driver for the motivation for **Streaming in Heaven's Flow**. For a life to be given fully to worship, prayer and music, there has to be a greater understanding of intimacy with God and His desire to be with us. Otherwise, we approach the doing of spiritual things as workers and not lovers.

A. The Intimacy Factor

The Amplified Bible's version of John 1:18 (above) is very enlightening. The intimacy between God the Father and God the Son is clearly defined. If we follow the point all the way through, this is the **intimacy factor** that can carry through to our lives before the Lord. Very few people will ever sustain long-term prayer and intercession without the grasp of the power of this intimacy.

We are privileged to be a part of what the Father has with the Son, and the Son has with the Father. Intimacy with God helps us walk a powerful, constant Christian life.

B. The Intimate Friendship of the Holy Spirit

> **2 Corinthians 13:14** - *The amazing grace of the Master, Jesus Christ,*
> *the extravagant love of God, the **intimate friendship** of the Holy Spirit,*
> *be with all of you.* (MSG)

Love with no fear and open intimacy are major connections to the heart of God. And from the power of His presence love exudes in both directions. Many people haven't received the message of intimacy and love because they have never seen it modeled. Intimacy in the realm of prayer and worship is a great facilitator (helper).

> **John 15:5** - *"I am the Vine, you are the branches. When you're joined with Me and I with*
> *you, the relation **intimate** and organic, the harvest is sure to be abundant.*
> *Separated, you can't produce a thing."* (MSG)

4. There is No Fear in the Perfect Love of God

> **I John 4:18** - *There is no room in love for fear. Well-formed love **banishes** fear.*
> *Since fear is crippling, a fearful life-fear of death,*
> *fear of judgment is one not yet fully formed in love.* (MSG)

Fear is an evil taskmaster. There are so many people that don't live out the fullness of their lives because of fear. Fear produces lack of confidence, insecurity, nightmares, a certain withdrawal from reality. Whereas love produces strength, hope, faith, joy, and an ongoing endurance. Perfect love casts out, annihilates, and makes fear go away.

1 John 4:16 - 19

[16] *We have come to know and have believed the **love** which God has for us.*
*God is **love**, and the one who abides in love abides in God, and God abides in him.*

[17] *By this, love is perfected with us, so that we may have confidence in the day of judgment; because as He is, so also are we in this world.*

[18] *There is **no fear** in love; because God's perfect love drives out fear.* (NCV)
because fear has torment [in it], it involves judgment
and the one who fears is not perfected in love.

*has not reached the full **maturity** of love*
[is not yet grown into love's complete perfection]. (AMP, KJV, NLT)

[19] *We love, because He first loved us.* (NAS)

The Word of God helps us with the deeper revelation of why He loves us, why we can return love to Him freely and unconditionally and not be afraid. Start again, because of love, to open your heart, to flow in worship . . . to engage in prayer . . . to read His Word and allow the cleansing that it brings. God is love.

There is **no fear** in love; but perfect love casts out (all) fear.

"God's love translated onto the human plane is like the ocean,
wave after wave, never stopping, never having to restart itself again."

5. For The Lord's Pleasure all Things are Created, Especially You

Years ago, at a youth conference in Arkansas, I was with a team of very powerful leaders. After two and half days of meetings in the presence of the Lord and many changed lives, we were tearing down the sound system and carrying it to the waiting van.

This young worship leader, as we were loading the van, said, "Yeah isn't it awesome, all things were created for His pleasure. Kent, your voice was created for His pleasure. You're hands that play the guitar were created for His pleasure. Your whole life and your heart were created for His pleasure."

A. For Your Pleasure, Lord, - Because of Your Desire

Revelation 4:11 - *Thou art worthy, O Lord, to receive glory honor and power: for thou hast created all things, and **for Thy pleasure** they are and were created.* (KJV)

*" for you created all things, and because of **your desire** they existed, and were created."* (WEB)

This conversation changed my life forever. It really wrecked my life for two or three weeks. I kept thinking, "I am not playing my music just for people, I play my music unto the Lord because of love. I keep singing even when I am tired because of love."

All Things were Created for His Pleasure, Especially YOU! Through the 40 years of ministry, I have said that I would not ever work this hard for any man on the earth. But I would for Jesus because of love. In the end, He is worthy of it all.

The Greek word for pleasure is: thelēma - (the'-lā-mä) - meaning the purpose of God to bless mankind through Christ. It is our Heavenly Father's choice,

His desire and for **His pleasure** that He made us for love, for friends and a family.

Philippians 2:13 - *. . for it is God who is at work in you, both to will and to work for* **His good pleasure** *[and satisfaction and delight].* (NAS, AMP)

Revelations and Thoughts: _____

_____

Study, Discuss and Think About: Lover's will always outwork workers, because of love.

* The reason that we worship is because of Love. The reason that we pray is because of Love. The power to sustain a lifestyle of worship and prayer comes from the bas_____ of tr_____ love.

* Learning the deeper realm of intimacy: 2 Corinthians 13:14 talks about the intimate friendship of the Holy Spirit after mentioning the extravagant love of God.

  Write down the importance of intimacy and the realm of friendship as you see or feel it. Recall a time where intimacy or friendship in real life experience made a huge difference in somebody's life.

* Fear is an evil task master. Fear produces lack of confidence, insecurity and nightmares. Perfect love casts out, annihilates and makes fear go away. Why is there no room for fear in love?

Every Believer's Eternal Identity
Royal Priests unto the Lord

One day, as we were leaving the Prayer Room, I asked Jim Stern, my son-in-law, a question. We had just finished three hours of prayer and worship from 9 a.m. until noon, and we were headed out to lunch.

As we were packing up our instruments, I said to Jim, "What is the greatest truth that has never been taught to the American church believer?" He said, "That's fairly simple. It is the missing truth: Every believer's eternal identity; we **are** the Royal Priesthood."

1. Every Believer is Part of God's Priesthood - I Peter 2:9

Revelation 5:9 - 10 Our Eternal Identity in Christ: beyond our earthly identity

> *And they sang a new song, saying, "Worthy are You to take the book and to break its seals; for you were slain, and purchased for God with Your blood*
>> *men from every tribe and tongue and people and nation."*
>
> [10] *"You have made them to be a kingdom and **priests** to our God; and they will reign upon the earth."*
>
> *And You have made them a kingdom (**royal race**) and priests to our God, and they shall reign [**as kings**] over the earth.* (AMP)

We must know that priesthood is our God-given eternal identity in Christ.

A. Kingly Priesthood ... a kingdom of priests ... a spiritual house of Holy Priests

I Peter 2:5, 9, 10

> *You also, as living stones, are being built up as a spiritual house for a holy priesthood, to offer up spiritual sacrifices acceptable to God through Jesus Christ.*
>
> [9] *But you are A CHOSEN RACE, A ROYAL PRIESTHOOD, A HOLY NATION,*
> *A PEOPLE FOR God's OWN POSSESSION,*
> *so that you may proclaim the excellencies of Him who has called you out of darkness into His marvelous light;*
>
> [10] *for you once were NOT A PEOPLE, but now you are THE PEOPLE OF GOD; you had NOT RECEIVED MERCY, but now you have RECEIVED MERCY.*

B. For We Will Function as Priests

in a holy priesthood even in eternity. Our priestly identity causes us to have greater light and revelation of who we are and why we pray and worship.

Isaiah 61:6

> *But you will be called the **priests** of the LORD; You will be spoken of as **ministers** of our God. You will eat the wealth of nations, and in their riches you will boast.*

2. Our Identity in Christ: the Four Major Parts

A. Chosen - selected by the Lord Himself. We can say that a praying church is many people, united by the Blood of Jesus, who gather together with a common goal.

B. Royal Priesthood - 1) You were made to serve in the inner courts of our King.
2) Worship and prayer is your spiritual service of worship.

C. Holy Nation - You develop a greater understanding of what holiness is. Your worldly desires for sin fade away and you long for the things that God longs for in His heart.

D. His Own Possession - *We are the people that belong to God. We were purchased by the Blood to show forth His perfections, to display His virtues. We are living testimonies of the goodness of God. He claimed us as **His own possession**.* (ERV)

> **Exodus 19:6** - *And you shall be to Me a kingdom of priests and a holy nation. These are the words that you shall speak to the sons of Israel.*

 Revelations and Thoughts: _____

_____

3. The Forever Priesthood

> **Hebrews 7:2-3**
>
> (Melchizedek) *king of **righteousness**, and then also king of **Salem**, which is king of **peace**.*
>
> *Without father, without mother, without genealogy, having neither beginning of days nor end of life, but made like the Son of God, he remains a **priest perpetually**.*

A. The Attributes and Meaning of Melchizedek

1. His name translated means the "king of righteousness."

2. Further, he was referred to as the king of Salem, which literally means the "king of peace." Only Jesus is referred to by these names in both Testaments.

3. This king was without father and without mother and even without genealogy. (For a normal king, this is not humanly possible.)

Think about this! Priesthood and priestly ministry do not go away in eternity.

4. The Priestly Ministry of Prayer and Worship

A. Every Believer - a Priestly Lifestyle

> **I Peter 2:5** - *We are living stones, being built up as a **spiritual** house for a holy **priesthood**, to offer up **spiritual** sacrifices acceptable to God through Jesus Christ.*

B. Spiritual Offerings are Simply Our Music, Our Worship, and Our Prayers

These all become a type of spiritual warfare. We have been given the most valuable and powerful tool. The Living Word, set to music, sung from hearts on fire, is a pure, righteous, spiritual force!!

5. Offerings in the Holy Spirit

I Peter 2: 4 - *You as living stones, a holy order of priests, making those offerings of the Spirit which are pleasing to God though Jesus Christ.* (BBE)

This is what He said we would do . . . making offerings in the Holy Spirit. He has taken us His friends, His Bride and His Army. We are serving as Priests first to the Lord, secondly as ministers, acting as His care-givers (helpers) to all people.

Revelations and Thoughts: _____

_____

Study, Discuss and Think About: Every believers eternal identity - Priests to the Lord

❖ In I Peter 2:9 it clearly states that we are four distinct things as New Testament believers. List them below.

1.

2.

3.

4.

❖ The powerful person and qualities of the Lord Jesus are displayed in Hebrews 7:2-3. Most commentators say that when Melchizedek appeared to Abraham in Genesis 14:18 it is the pre-incarnate Christ appearing in the Old Testament. He was establishing the true line of a Holy Priesthood.

What is the meaning of the name Melchizedek?

What three attributes of Melchizedek established the Forever Priesthood?

1.

2.

3.

❖ It is a great honor to be a part of fulfilling the Priestly Ministry of worship and intercession. Our spiritual offerings are simply our m_____, our w_____ and our p_____.

Intercession: The Power to Intervene
History Belongs to the Intercessor

Everyone is called to **"pray more"** and pray consistently until we see a greater release of the Lord's anointing, the Lord's help and His justice on the earth.

1. Intercession: History Belongs to the Intercessor

I visited a church in Littleton, Colorado to do Night of Worship for a church there. Upon arriving early in the afternoon, the doors were locked (I had driven from Colorado Springs), I looked in the front window.

On the archway going into the sanctuary, in bold block letters, it said,
"History belongs to the intercessor. "

I was stunned, and stood amazed at this statement. It changed my life forever, for it summed up what I had come to believe was the mission and purpose of every believer. Everyone is called to **"pray more"** and pray consistently until we see a greater release of the Lord's anointing, the Lord's help and His justice on the earth.

2. Make Up the Hedge and Stand in the Gap Against Injustice
God is looking for someone to stand up for what's right.

Ezekiel 22:29 - 31

29 *The people of the land have: Practiced oppression and committed robbery, and they have wronged the poor and needy and have oppressed the sojourner without justice.*

30 ***I searched** for **a man** among them who would **make up the hedge** (KJV) and **stand in the gap before Me** for the land, so that I would not destroy it; but I found no one (not one).*

30 *I looked for someone to stand up for Me against all this (injustice)
to repair the defenses of the city, to take a stand for Me*

*. . . and stand in the gap to protect this land so I wouldn't have to destroy it.
I couldn't find anyone.   Not one.* (MSG)

31 *Thus I have poured out My indignation on them; I have consumed them with the fire of My wrath; their way I have brought upon their heads, declares the Lord GOD.*

The injustice that we see on the earth right now will not go on forever. Jesus is coming back again and the fact of the matter is that His very Throne is established on righteousness and justice. We are becoming the people of prayer, worship and justice.

3. Those Who Partner with God

"Those who **partner** with **God,** to bring about His will and Kingdom on the earth, are **shaping** the **future** through prayer and intercession." Carla Henry

The real understanding of intercession as found in the Hebrew language is very clear. The following three actions take guts, courage, and a certain selflessness. This is in the heart of those actively doing the priestly ministry of prayer and worship. Check out these definitions.

4. Intercede - to intervene; to pray; mediate; (step in, insert [yourself], interject)

A. Step in - [to help] . . . this is a decision of our will, we have a choice.

B. Insert - yourself means we are believing for His help and covering. Some risk is involved.

C. Interject - (squeeze in, get in between);
Squeeze in between good and evil as an intercessor.
Numbers 21:4 - 7

The people of God are impatient in their journey through the desert, and of course they start complaining big-time. The Lord sent serpents in their midst for the sin of disrespect. Realizing their sin, they said to Moses

"We have sinned, because we have spoken against the LORD and you; * ***intercede with the LORD**, that He may remove the serpents from us."*   And **Moses interceded** *for the people.*

(*intercede: this is the first time this word appears in the Bible and it happens twice in the same verse.)

5. They Pleaded for an Intercessor

A. The **Situation:** (verse 4) - *"The Israelites set out from Mount Hor by the way of the Red Sea, to go around the land of Edom; and the people became **impatie**nt because of the journey."*

Other translations say, *"The soul of the people was short, people complaining again."*

B. The **Attitude:** (verse 5) - *The people spoke against God and Moses, "Why have you brought us up out of Egypt to die in the wilderness? For there is no food and no water, and we loathe this miserable food."*

They were accusatory in nature and disrespectful of authority.
Loathe: to dislike greatly and often with disgust or intolerance, to detest
[The word loathe by its very nature reveals the attitude of their heart in that moment.]

C. The **Judgment:** (verse 6) - *"The LORD sent fiery serpents among the people and they bit the people, so that many people of Israel died."*

Old Testament judgment was seemingly very severe, but the Lord knew the importance of obedience and the right heart attitude. Because these two things define the degree of the people's blessing.

D. The **Remedy:** (verse 7) - *"So the people came to Moses and said, "We have sinned, because we have spoken against the LORD and you "intercede* with the Lord, that He may remove the serpents from us." And **Moses interceded** for the people.*

Here we are, in the Lord, able to intercede and intervene while covered with His awesome protection: **a.** His Name **b.** His Blood and **c.** the power of His life as the Crucified Lamb.

 Revelations and Thoughts: _____

6. Because of Intercession

Because of intercession, **disaster** can be **averted**. Because some one prays, tragedy can be knocked out. This should give us a clue to the importance of the life of someone living right before the Lord, living in a place to be a mouthpiece of the Lord, praying on the earth. The beginning of the element of intercession is found early in the Bible. It is brought forth in the Old Testament, the Five Books of Moses, (The Torah). It is first in the book of Numbers.

It is possible . . . to interceded with the Lord, to intervene in the affairs of God and men.
It is possible . . . to step in between, mediate,
and the change the outcome by righteous intercession.

A. God's Desire is to have Many Intercessors

There is a direct connection between us praying in the will of God and the release of His justice on the earth. Prayer and intercession take deeper root in our hearts when the understanding that God makes wrong things right hits home. It's fairly apparent to me now that more people would run to the place of prayer and intercession if they knew the significant results. Every breath we take and every word we speak in intercession is causing justice and righteousness to be established.

Isaiah 59:14 - 17

[14] *Justice is turned back*, *and righteousness stands far away;*
For truth has stumbled in the street, and uprightness cannot enter.
[15] *Yes, truth is lacking; and he who turns aside from evil makes himself a prey.*
*Now the LORD saw, and it was displeasing in His sight that **there was no justice**.*
[16] *And He saw that there was **no man**, and was astonished that there was **no one to intercede**;*
Then His own arm brought salvation to Him, and His righteousness upheld Him.
[17] *He put on righteousness like a breastplate, and a helmet of salvation on His head;*
*And He put on garments of vengeance for clothing and wrapped Himself with **zeal as a mantle**.*

This is truly a sad story unfolding in chapter 59 of Isaiah. The scripture records that God has written the Law on every man's heart. Everyone has a conscience and a sense of right and wrong. "Justice was turned back and righteousness stood far away" because enough people denied what they knew to be the truth concerning right and wrong.

The quote goes like this, "All that is necessary for the triumph of evil is that
good men and women do nothing."
[Edmund Burke (January 12, 1729 – July 9, 1797) was an Irish political philosopher, Whig politician and statesman who is often regarded as the father of modern conservatism.]

Concerning prayer, this is also the truth. All it takes for evil to conquer a nation is that the Christians never pray and live a life of ease and comfort.

 Revelations and Thoughts: _____

_____

Study, Discuss and Think About: God is looking for someone. Will He find you?

* Give an example of how you have had to stand up for justice and against injustice in your life.

* How can we use our tongue for the power of blessing? (example: encouragement, compliments, etc.) List out the forms of speaking and words that do not bring a blessing.

* Our Test: keep track for one day, the five most positive / negative things that you say out loud.

Prophetic Worship and Intercession

1. Releasing the powerful voice of the Lord that changes hearts and minds.

2. We allow the Lord to sing and play through us as His holy vessels.

3. We then do music and singing that is touched and directed by the Lord's anointing.

[All of these facilitate spontaneous flow that releases the power of the Word of God.]

1. Releasing the Voice of the Lord - Psalm 29:3 - 9

There is a great need for the continuous release of the voice of the Lord in worship, music and our appointed times of prayer!! We are His people, set in this kingdom place to sing, to worship, to intercede, giving the voice of the Lord its rightful place on the earth and in spiritual warfare in the heavenlies.

Psalm 29:3 - 9

The voice of the Lord is on many waters the God of glory thunders,
The voice of the LORD is powerful; the voice of the LORD is majestic.
The voice of the LORD hews out flames of fire. The voice of the LORD makes
the deer to calve, and strips the forests bare; and in His temple everything says, "Glory!"

2. We Allow the Lord to Sing and Play through Us as His Holy Vessels

As we are surrendered to Him with consecrated hearts and lives, He pours Himself through us as His **vessels.** While we are singing, worshipping and praying, God uses us as friends, co-laborers and voices for releasing His heart and purposes.

2 Corinthians 4:6 - 7 It's you and me Streaming in Heaven's flow.

[6] For God, who said, "Light shall shine out of darkness, "is the One who has shone in our hearts to give the Light of the knowledge of the glory of God in the face of Christ.
*[7] But we have this **treasure** in **earthen vessels**.*

3. We Do Music and Singing Touched and Directed by the Lord's Anointing

We have received **an anointing** from the Holy One.

We are a spiritual reservoir, a holding place for the Holy Spirit. In this anointing, the abiding power of the Holy Spirit, will cause us to know all things, in time.
The Holy Spirit leads and guides us into all the truth so walk as Spirit-led believers.

I John 2:20, 27

*"But **you have an anointing** from the Holy One, and you know all things...*
*besides you hold your anointing from the **Holy One**." (BER)*
*[27] But the anointing which you have received of Him **abides in you**,*
and you need not that any man teach you,
*but as **the** same **anointing teaches you** of all things, and is truth and is not a lie,*
even as it's taught you, and you shall abide in Him.

4. Prophetic Worship and Singing:
Bubble Up Like Springs and Fountains (like in Lesson 6)

prophesy - naba' - [nä·vä'] - to prophesy under influence of divine spirit

> to cause to **bubble up** . . . (fountains, gurgling streams);
> to **pour forth** words abundantly as it done by those who speak or [sing] with passion or divine emotion of mind or heart

This definition of the prophetic is simple to do and understand. The Lord intended that every believer would speak by inspiration of their own heart. They would live under the divine inspiration of the Holy Spirit. It applies to our everyday life and all that we do in it.

prophesy - nabiy' - [nä·vē'] - those actuated (moved to action) by the divine Spirit.
> spokesman, speaker, prophet: prophecy, them that prophesy.

5. Prophetic Worship Outlined - I Chronicles 25:1 - 7

*Moreover, David and the commanders of the army set apart for the **[temple] service** some of the sons of Asaph and of Heman and of Jeduthun, who were to **prophesy** with lyres, harps and cymbals: and the sons of Asaph under Asaph's direction **prophesied** according to the direction of the **King**.*

*under the direction of their **father** Jeduthun with the harp,*
> *who **prophesied** in giving thanks and praising the LORD.*

*Heman, the King's seer, all the sons of Heman to exalt him according to the **words of God** . . . All these were under the direction of their father for the **music***
> *in the house of the Lord . . . were instructed in the **songs** of the **Lord**.*

*[7]Their number who were **trained in singing** to the **LORD**,*
> *with their relatives, all who were **skillful**, was 288.*

Four Strategic Points: These help our understanding of prophetic worship and its flow.

These will help us maintain focus . . . on the why and destination of prophetic worship. God has always used ordinary people to be involved in His extraordinary things.

1. **Act**: . . . Who were **to prophesy!** [Those who are to proclaim God's messages.]

2. **Create** the Base: . . . Prophesy **with music,** provide the **accompaniment** for voices, lyrics and melodies that become a foundation for prophetic release.

3. **Know** the Purpose: . . . **To minister** - first to the Lord, ministry before the Lord, giving Him the glory, honor and praise (devotion, adoration). Then ministry to His people will be stronger because you've been with Him.

4. **Live The Lifestyle and Follow Through**: . . . The singers and musicians were **set apart**, separated, playing and singing from a place of full attention and surrender. They did it: actively doing priestly ministry, places a demand on your own gifting in God's anointing, step-out of the fear zone and "try it"**!!!**

Flowing in New Songs and Songs of the Holy Spirit
Training Singers and Musicians

1. Breaking Out in Spiritual Songs

2. Drink Deeply of God's Spirit and Sing Holy Songs of Praise

3. 150 Psalms for Singing Until Jesus Comes Back Again!

Breaking out of the box of "regular" singing and playing, and the normal order of a set list is so very freeing. Don't be afraid to experiment, jump out, try your wings and fly.

1. Breaking Out in Spiritual Songs

Spiritual songs are songs generated from the hearts of believers who are touched by the power of the Holy Spirit.
This is one of the coolest forms of singing and music ever.
It releases a singer from singing a fully written out set of lyrics to a prewritten melody. This is some of the most enjoyable singing a singer can ever do on the earth. It's like creating art on the fly. It's like a toddler doing finger painting.

The song and the lyrics are created from the spiritual flow, the energy and the emotion of the moment the singer is singing in. The same is true for musicians. In place of lyrics, they are playing a river of music notes over chord progressions that are free flowing from their hands and their heart. It is so very freeing and the sense of fulfillment is most times overwhelming.

> **Ephesians 5:19**
>
> But **drink deeply** of God's Spirit. **Speak out** to one another in psalms and hymns and spiritual songs, joining with one another in **holy songs** of praise and **of the Spirit**,
>
> **using your voice** in songs and making melody in your heart to the Lord; (BBE)

2. Drink Deeply of God's Spirit and Sing Holy Songs of Praise

I want to point out these two categories from Ephesians 5. The first is drink deeply of God's Spirit. The second is holy songs of praise and holy songs of the Spirit. These are really important because many singers and musicians have been trained only in performance based music and singing. The tendency is to do exactly what is set before them on the music sheet.

These two categories give us the freedom to venture out to sing more from our hearts than from our minds. It's found and accessed much more in the Presence based orientation. The anchor point is the same for all of us.

We are singing and praying the Word of God with all of our heart engaged. All while our minds are creating spontaneous melodies and lyrics. It's truly making use of this type of singing called holy songs of praise, songs and music that are generated by the Holy Spirit.

A. Spiritual Songs in the Prayer Room

The use of spiritual songs in the Prayer Room is one of our greatest foundational tools. I know there are people reading this study guide right now that may be freaking out at this concept. But singers regardless of their training, can adapt to this natural well of creativity that is within them.

So when the opportunity arises, give it your best shot. You can start by doing training sessions that help people match their melodies to the chord progression that is being played. Little by little, you will become more comfortable with doing it and actually become very proficient at it.

Revelations and Thoughts: _____

_____

_____

3. 150 Psalms for Singing Until Jesus Comes Back Again!

This so important too for all of us to understand. There are 150 songs which are now 150 Psalms canonized in our Bible. People have been singing these for over 3,000 years. They have every aspect of life, up and down, telling about of the condition of the heart of man on their worst days and their best days.

Here's what Matthew Henry's Commentary says about the Psalms:

The singing of psalms is a **teaching** ordinance as well as a **praising** ordinance.
We are not only to quicken and encourage ourselves, but to *teach and admonish one another,* mutually excite our **affections**, and convey instructions.

When we sing psalms, we make no melody unless we sing with grace in our hearts, (because) we are suitably affected by what we sing. We go along in it with true devotion and understanding. Psalms, hymns and spiritual songs are suited to special occasions, instead of their lewd and profane songs in their idolatrous worship.

4. The Treasury of David

Acts 13:22

> *After He had removed him, He raised up David to be their king, concerning whom*
> *He also testified and said, I HAVE FOUND DAVID, the son of Jesse,*
> *A MAN AFTER MY HEART, who will do all MY will.*

Years ago, a great man of God wrote a book called "The Treasury of David." His name is Charles Spurgeon (1834-1892), born in Essex, England. Of all his writings, the one that is his greatest work is "The Treasury of David," composed and polished over the span of nearly half his ministry. He first published this treasury in weekly installments over a twenty-year span in the London Metropolitan Tabernacle's periodical, The Sword and the Trowel.

Within a decade more than 120,000 sets had been sold. The Treasury of David is a superb literary achievement. Eric Hayden, pastor of the Metropolitan Tabernacle a century after Spurgeon's ministry began there, calls this work "Spurgeon's magnum opus." Spurgeon's wife said that if Spurgeon had never written any other work, this would have been a permanent literary memorial.

Revelations and Thoughts: _____

Study, Discuss and Think About:

⋄ Breaking out into spiritual songs is one of the coolest forms of singing. Ephesians 5:19 says this "but drink de_____ of God's Spirit. Sp_____ out to one another in psalms, hymns and spiritual songs joi_____ with one another in holy so_____ of praise and of the Spirit."

⋄ Why are spiritual songs important in the Prayer Room?

⋄ Name three ways can we fulfill Acts 13:22 in our own lives, becoming like David who was called a man after God's own heart.

1.

2.

3.

If My People . . . Called by My Name . . . Humble Themselves

This teaching begins explaining the nine elements of 2 Chronicles 7:14. This is God's call to all of His people Old or New Testament. This is a lifestyle that will represent Jesus to a lost and searching world.

1. When the People of God - actually humble themselves and pray - 2 Chronicles 7:12-16

This is one of the greatest promises the Lord has ever afforded mankind. It is direct, it is to the point and you can't kill it even with your procrastination and laziness. He left no room to wiggle out of this obedience and the resultant fruit if we obey.

> **2 Chronicles 7:12-16   Setting the Standards . . .**
>
> [12] *Then the LORD appeared to Solomon at night and said to him,*
>   *"I have heard your prayer and have chosen this place for Myself as a house of sacrifice.*
>
> [13] *If I shut up the heavens so that there is no rain, or if I command the locust to devour the land, or if I send pestilence among My people,*
>
> [14] *and* (1) **My people** *who are* (2) **called** *by My name* (3) **humble** *themselves*
>
>   *and* (4) **pray** *and* (5) **seek** *My face and* (6) **turn** *from their wicked ways,*
>
>   *then* (7) *I will* **hear** *from heaven,* (8) **forgive** *their sin and* (9) **heal** *their land.*
>
> [15] *Now My eyes will be open and My ears attentive to the* **prayer offered** *in this place.*
>
> [16] *For now I have chosen and consecrated this house that My name may be there forever, and My eyes and* **My heart** *will be there perpetually."*

2. Living as the People Called by His Name

This is the identity of every believer. Our place, position is to function in priestly ministry as:

A. Devoted Worshippers (2 Corinthians 11:3)

> *But [now] I am fearful, lest that even as the serpent beguiled Eve by his cunning, so your minds may be corrupted and seduced from wholehearted and sincere and pure devotion to Christ.*

B. Dedicated Intercessors (Hebrews 7:25)

A prayer and worship culture is a major fix for prayerlessness. We are to become a people who are skillful at using His Name in worship, warfare and intercession. It makes us uniquely different from the people of this world and its culture.

 Revelations and Thoughts: _____

_____

3. Explaining the Nine Elements of 2 Chronicles 7:14

(1) **My People** . . . we actually belong to the Lord. It means that you actually belong to God and you act like it. You can not expect to live R rated lifestyles and expect to flow in the holiness of God. Look in the mirror, and say, "I am a part of God's people. My identity is with God's people."

(2) **Called by My Name** . . . this is a special class and category.
There is a name higher that you are called by, the name of the Lord, the name of Jesus, the name "the Body of Christ. "You act differently when you are called by this name. You see and perceive differently because you are in this special class and category. You are a person called by the Living God's Name.

(3) **Humble Themselves** . . . it is the choice of your heart and will. **I Peter 5:5**
God is opposed to the proud, but gives grace to the humble. This scripture reveals the desire of the heart of the Father: humility, lowly and meek. In God's plan, He knew humility would be attractive to every generation. So humility and being humble is one of God's all time principles on how we should walk in this life.

4. Praying, Seeking and Turning From

(4) **Pray** . . . get started, don't punk out now. We know He does hear and He will answer. Pray and sing the Word of God out loud, putting the Lord in remembrance of what He said He would do. The Lord actually enjoys this greatly; that we would so cherish the Bible, the Living Word that we would use His Word as a strong foundation for what we are praying and how we are praying.

(5) **Seek My Face** . . . This should be our lifetime pursuit.
Is this not the love of your life, to seek the Face of the Lord? He is beautiful beyond description, beauty, splendor and majesty are before His throne.

I am sure there are times that I have sought the Lord just for the fact that as I press in, I will certainly receive a greater light and revelation concerning His awesome beauty. It carries in its words the longing and yearning of the human heart for something more than we currently have. Seeking the Lord has become a lifetime pursuit for me.

(6) **Turn from Their Wicked Ways** . . . Turn to the Lord, it's truly our only hope.
Turn to the Lord and turn from your wicked ways. I have been hearing this for months now, "Kent, tell the people in your Nation to turn to Me, tell the government officials to turn to Me, tell your educators and school officials **this is the time** to turn to Me." It is super important that we act now; hearts surrendered, we are seeking the wisdom of an infinite God.

Revelations and Thoughts: _____

_____

_____

5. God's Promise: He will . . . Hear, Forgive and Heal Our Land

(7) **I will Hear from Heaven** . . . Will we or will we not take advantage of this promise?

Thank You, thank You, thank You Lord. You spoke it out loud. You spoke it in real time. "I w-i-l-l h-e-a-r f-r-o-m H-e-a-v-e-n." Oh Happy Day. So will we or will we not take advantage of these words from our Heavenly Father?

I wrote a song years ago, it was entitled, "Are You Listening With Your Heart." So many people today, want to know the answer to this question. And further, their first question is "is anybody really listening to what I am trying to say."

(8) **Forgive Their Sin** . . . The great miracle, it's a launch pad for spiritual endeavors.

This one is the greatest miracle to me. The forgiveness of sins can only be done by Almighty God. I like it when my sins are forgiven. It accomplishes all these things: my conscience doesn't bother me any more; my heart is lifted by the fresh wind of God in my spirit. It's a place of true purity because of the power of spiritual cleansing. It's a launch pad for spiritual endeavors.

Daniel 11:32 *"...but the people who know their God shall be strong, and carry out great exploits."*

(9) **Heal Their Land** . . . from devastation and pestilence to restoration and abundant life

When God heals something, it is healed for real. He makes all things new and where there was devastation and pestilence He brings abundant life and restoration for all to see. Lord we want this America and this American Land healed. Please Lord, heal our land. Only a giant God, only a big, big God can save us now. Only the Lord, the Holy and the Lord of all Glory can help us now.

 Revelations and Thoughts: _____

Study, Discuss and Think About:

❖ In 2 Chronicles 7:12 - 16 in your opinion list the top three elements of the nine listed within that Scripture and include a simple explanation of "why."

❖ What are the reasons that people don't engage in becoming devoted worshippers or dedicated intercessors?

❖ God gave us a promise that He will **hear** from Heaven, **forgive** our sins and **heal** our land. In 2 Chronicles 7:14. To you, which is the greatest miracle out of these three things that God has promised and offered to do?

I realize that this is really a difficult question but it is so good for us to think and process through it.

Section

Three

Lessons 13 - 18 on intermingling praise with prayer and worship with intercession

The Weapons of Our Spiritual Warfare are Mighty

1. Worshipping Intercessors functioning as Prayer Warriors . . .

Divinely Powerful (by the Lord Himself). . . are the weapons of our warfare.
Spiritual Warfare . . . is what believers do as spiritual warriors and intercessors.

God made sure that we would not be left defenseless or unable to pray and do His work. The cost of the sacrifice of the Lord Jesus on the Cross was so substantial, our heavenly Father made sure in His overall plan that it would count at the highest levels. This plan involves us taking our place on the earth, as worshipping intercessors and those who wield the sword spiritually.

The passage of scripture below is really unsurpassed in its clarity and definition of spiritual warfare. It is worth extra time and attention, (study, meditation), to attain the deeper parts of the revelation of God concerning every believer, as His priests, actively operating in worship and intercession.

2. The Weapons of Our Warfare are Mighty

2 Corinthians 10:3 - 5

3 *For though we walk in the flesh, we do not war according to the flesh,*

4 *for **the weapons of our warfare** (the arms of our knighthood) are not of the flesh,*
        *but **divinely powerful** for the destruction of fortresses,*

(for the weapons of our warfare not carnal,
        *but **mighty through God** to the **pulling down** of strongholds).*

5 *We are destroying speculations and every lofty thing raised up against the knowledge of God,*
and we are taking every thought captive to the obedience of Christ. (NAS, WYC, KJV)

a. Our warfare is fought in the Spirit Realm not in the flesh.

b. These weapons are divinely powerful and mighty through God.

c. Our battle is stopping all that is exalting itself against the true knowledge of God.

d. Worship, prayer and music are used for the destruction of spiritual strongholds.

3. Our Warfare: It is Fought in the Spirit Realm . . . verse 3

Not warring after the flesh, we are fighting with His strength. It would be futile to use natural weapons against spiritual enemies. If you set off a nuclear bomb next to an angel's head, guess what happens? Nothing, for angels exist and are living in another realm.

*For though we walk in the flesh, we do **not war according to** the flesh.* (NAS)
*Weak men, we may be, but it is not as such that **we fight** our battles.* (NEB)
*Human indeed we are, but **it is in no human strength** that we fight our battles.* (KNOX)

As we enter into deep worship and intercession, we move right into the middle of God's power realm. In this realm **His royal authority rules**. Intercessors with this authority **overcome** from the prayer room.

4. Our Weapons are Spiritual Weapons that are Divinely Powerful

A. The Arms of Our Knighthood ... verse 4a

*For the weapons of our warfare (**arms of** our **knighthood**) are not of the flesh.* (WYC)
*Our tools are ready at hand for **clearing** the ground of **every obstruction** and **building lives** of obedience into maturity.* (MSG)

There is unlimited power and strength available in the Lord of Hosts. He is the God of angel armies. There are no power shortages with Him. When we engage with the strength of His presence and these spiritual weapons, we are a formidable force.

B. Our Weapons are Absolutely Mighty ... verse 4b

Darkness **is dispelled** and evil destroyed by this power.

... but divinely powerful for the destruction of fortresses. (NAS)

This power ruptures and defeats the kingdom of darkness.

*But they are **mighty before God** for the overthrow and destruction of strongholds ... but they are **divinely potent** to demolish strongholds.* (NEB)

These are weapons, **absolutely mighty** because they are **empowered** by God.

 Revelations and Thoughts: _____

_____

5. Our Battle is Stopping anything Exalting Itself against the Knowledge of God

The Lord takes His sword in His right hand and knights you into the greater ministry of His command and dominion. Most believers will start to know this anointing, as they move more into the place (lifestyle) of diligent prayer and worship.

Begin using everything (tools and weapons) God has provided in this spiritual arsenal.

A. We are Releasing God's Light and Truth Tenaciously, Without Fear - verse 5

Eliminating deceptive fantasies. The conceits of men try to **hide** the truth of God.

*Our battle is to **bring down** every deceptive fantasy and every imposing defense that men erect against the true knowledge of God.* (Phi)

*Yes, **we can pull down** the conceits of men and every barrier of pride which set itself up against the true knowledge of God.* (KNOX)

This is our battle everyday and this is why we pray and intercede for the freedom of every man. Professing themselves to be wise, they became fools. For God has used the weak things of this world to confound the mighty.

> *We use our powerful God-tools for **smashing warped philosophies**.* (MSG)
>
> *. . . and we are taking every thought captive to the obedience of Christ.* (NAS)
> *We compel every human thought to surrender, come under the authority of Christ.* (NEB, Bas.)

Do we get it yet?

We must see intercession and worship for what God intended them to be: working prayer tools for building and awesome weapons for binding the kingdom of darkness.

 Revelations and Thoughts: _____

_____

6. Weapons That Release God's Help and Power

as We Enter into the Joy and Labor of Prayer and Worship

Spiritual, working tools for building
> (**praying, blessing,** and **releasing**),

yet powerful weapons for arresting the activities of darkness
> (**binding, stopping** and **destroying**).

A. The Word of God

It can't return void. Praying and singing releases its stored-up power.

> **Isaiah 55:11** - *So shall My word be that goes forth out of My mouth:*
> *it shall not return to Me **void**, but it shall accomplish that which I please,*
> *and it shall **prosper** in the thing for which I sent it.* (KJV)
>
> *. . . It will not return to Me **empty**, without accomplishing **what I desire**,*
> *and without succeeding in the matter for which I sent it.* (NAS)

Jesus is the Living Word. He is alive, therefore, the Word of God is alive. The power of the Word of God is defined this way in Hebrews 1:3, Jesus is the exact representation of the Father, He is the full radiance of the Father's glory. God's Word carries this power.

Hebrews 1:3

> *And He is the radiance of His glory and the exact representation of His nature, and upholds all things by the word of His power. When He had made purification of sins, He sat down at the right hand of the Majesty on high.*

B. Worship Itself is a Weapon

Enemies destroy themselves while Judah worshipped. The power of His Presence infused in His people's praise and worship is unstoppable.

2 Chronicles 20:18 - 25

18 Jehoshaphat bowed his head with his face to the ground, and **all (of) Judah** and the inhabitants of Jerusalem fell down before the LORD, **worshipping the LORD.**

19 The Levites, from the sons of the Kohathites and of the sons of the Korahites, stood up to praise the LORD God of Israel, with a **very loud voice.**

20 They rose early in the morning and went out to the wilderness of Tekoa; and when they went out, Jehoshaphat stood and said, "Listen to me, O Judah and inhabitants of Jerusalem, put your trust in the LORD your God and you will be **established.** Put your trust in His prophets and **succeed."**

21 When he (King Jehosaphat) had consulted with the people, he appointed those who **sang to the LORD** and those who **praised Him** in holy attire, as they **went out before the army** and said,   "Give thanks to the LORD, for His loving-kindness is everlasting."

22 When they **began singing and praising**, the **LORD set ambushes** against the sons of Ammon, Moab and Mount Seir, who had come against Judah; so they were struck down.

24 When Judah came to the lookout of the wilderness, they looked toward the multitude, and behold, they were corpses lying on the ground, and **no one had escaped.**

25 . . . Jehoshaphat and his people found much among them, goods, garments and valuable things more than they could carry. And they were three days **taking the spoil** because there was so much.

Honestly, can you imagine being called by your pastor to go out in front of the American military with only your voices and your little bitty harps? This is what happened to the Hebrew singers and musicians when King Jehosaphat had them lead the way into battle. That day the power of praise, worship and music, touched by His Presence won the battle.

 Revelations and Thoughts: _____

_____

Study, Discuss and Think About:

❖ On a scale of 1 - 10 (ten being the highest), how important is it that people see that every believer is called to high level prayer and worship, to actually function as prayer warriors?

❖ For though we walk in the fl_____, we do not w_____ according to the flesh. Human indeed we are, but it is in no hu_____ str_____ that we fight our battles.
. . . for the weapons of our warfare (a_____ of our kni_____) are not of the flesh but are divinely powerful.   (Fill in the blanks)

❖ Through the power of the anointing of God's presence, singing, worshipping and playing music unto the Lord becomes an unstoppable force.
Review 2 Chronicles 20:18 - 25. List out the top 3 most important points from this passage and write out a paragraph on each point.

Singing and Praying the Word of God

God's Word Will Not Return Void or Empty

Isaiah 55:11

*So will **My Word** be which goes forth from My mouth;*
*It will not return to Me **empty** (void), without accomplishing what I desire,*
and without succeeding in the matter for which I sent it.

*So is My word it **turns not** back unto Me empty, but has done that which I desired,*
*and prosperously **effected** that [for] which **I sent it**. (YLT)*

*It is the same with My word. I send it out, and it **always produces fruit**.*
It will accomplish all I want it to, it will prosper everywhere I send it. (NLT)

1. Learning the Bible by Singing Scripture Choruses

In the 1970's and 80's, we learned the Bible by singing Scripture choruses. There is probably no other way we would have known so much of the Bible without the power of singing the Word of God. Thousands of people from non-Bible reading backgrounds came into the greater depths of the Word because the Word was set to music.

In the same way today, the Scriptures are finding their way back into our church songs, our modern choruses and is a large part our time in the Prayer Room. We are so much stronger spiritually because we are singing and praying the Word of God.

People in third world countries have no problem singing the Word as long as they have Bibles in their possession. Singing and praying the Word of God is not based on having a high level education, financial status or social skills. It's based on their love for God, their hunger for the help of the Lord and their heart to see God's kingdom established in their region and city.

A. Psalms, Hymns and Spiritual Songs

This is the pattern now for the New Testament believers. I am sure that I would have never lasted in the pattern of Old Testament law and worship. Just imagine if you had to kill a bull or a goat and collect its blood and offer it as a sacrifice. I am not trying to gross you out but I want you to give thanks that Jesus shed His blood one time for you that you might have a new and living way into the presence of God.

Colossians 3:16 - *Let the **word of Christ** (our Lord) richly dwell within you, with all wisdom teaching and admonishing one another with*
***psalms**, (a song composed on a divine subject, in praise of God)*
***hymns**, (a song, an ode or a poem in honor of God put to music)*
***spiritual songs**, (songs generated from the heart, touched by the power of the Holy Spirit)*

*Let the teaching of Christ and His words keep on **living in you**. Keep on teaching and helping each other. Sing the **Songs of David** and the **church songs** and the **songs of Heaven** with hearts full of thanks to God.* (NLV)

 Revelations and Thoughts: _____

2. "I Will Sing of Your Word" - Singing the Scriptures

The Word of God plays an integral part in worship and prayer. The Hebrew understanding of singing and praying the Word comes from the tradition of how they sing and pray the Torah (the books of Moses, the first five books of our Bible).

Today the Jewish people are still singing and praying the Torah on the Western Wailing Wall in Jerusalem. At modern Synagogue services today, there is a **cantor** who sings and prays the Word leading the people to do the same. He is singing lines from Scriptural prayers of the Torah.

Psalm 119:171 – 172

[171] *Let my lips **utter praise**, for You teach me Your statutes.*

[172] *Let my tongue **sing of Your Word**, for all Your commandments are righteousness (justice).*
My tongue does sing of Thy saying(s), for all Thy commands [are] righteous. (YLT)

*My tongue shall sing [praise for the **fulfillment**] of Your word,*
for all Your commandments are righteous. (AMP)

*And let your promises **ring** from my tongue;* (MSG)　*Let me sing about your promises;* (NCV)

Sing of Your Word - [`anah] - to sing . . . utter tunefully . . . melodious: having a
pleasant melody. The primary meaning is to sing, hence to cry out our singing or cantor.

A focused effort to learn how to flow with worship into intercession will **benefit everybody**. Integrating the Word of God into our worship and prayer is super important because of its value and power.

3. God's People Singing and Praying the Bible

God's people singing and praying the Bible is a powerful force for the greater release of His Word, with His Light and Power on it. It is "Streaming in Heaven's Flow" of mercy, grace and justice and . . . faith.

Romans 10: 17 - *Faith comes by **hearing**, and hearing by the **Word of God**.*

The Living Word set to music, sung from hearts on fire,
it's a pure, righteous spiritual force!!

A. Praying and Singing the Word is a Crucial Stream, a Necessary Tool given by the Lord to fulfill Earth's Destiny

It is time to **refocus** on the very Book that the Lord left in our hands to be able to finish our prophetic journey. The Word helps us fulfill the awesome destiny He has given to each and every one. The power of the Word, the Light of the Word, the Holy Spirit revealing the Word of God is equipping us to do spiritual work. By its revelation, there can be no mistaking where we should be going and what we should be doing with our lives.

This is part of any corporate prayer and worship gathering because worship, prayer and music are working together. As your singers and musicians learn how to do this, three powerful things begin to happen:

❖ First, they are **releasing** the power of God's Word in a consistent and long-term manner.

❖ Second, they are using the Word of God to **bind up** principalities and powers of the kingdom of darkness.

❖ Third, they are learning, memorizing and getting the Scripture **deep** in their **hearts**.

I Peter 1 : 23 - *For you have been born again not of seed which is perishable but imperishable, that is, through the **living** and **enduring** Word of God.*

B. Holy Songs of Praise and Songs of the Spirit

One of the first categories of spiritual songs is holy songs of praise and the second is holy songs of the Spirit. This is really important because so many singers and musicians have been trained only in performance based music and singing. Their tendency is to do exactly what is set before them on the music sheet.

These two categories give us the freedom to venture out to sing more from our hearts than from our minds. It's found and accessed much more in the presence based orientation. The anchor point is the same for all of us.

We are singing and praying the Word of God with all of our heart engaged. All while our minds are creating spontaneous melodies and lyrics. It's truly making use of this type of singing called holy songs of praise, songs and music that are generated by the Holy Spirit.

Revelations and Thoughts: _____

_____

4. Breaking Out in Spiritual Songs

Spiritual songs are songs generated from the hearts of believers who are touched by the power of the Holy Spirit. This is one of the coolest forms of singing and music ever. It releases a singer from singing a fully written out set of lyrics to a prewritten melody.

This is some of the most enjoyable singing a singer can ever do on the earth. It's like creating art on the fly. It's like a toddler doing finger painting. The song and the lyrics are created from the spiritual flow, the energy and the emotion of the moment the singer is singing in.

The same is true for musicians. In place of lyrics, they are playing a river of music notes over chord progressions that are free flowing from their hands and their heart. It is so very freeing and the sense of fulfillment is most times overwhelming.

A. Jump into the Realm of Doing Worship, Prayer and Music

When the people of God begin to sing and pray the Scriptures, it releases the **stored up power** that is in the Word of God. I am thoroughly convinced that any person who knows Jesus and understands their salvation would immediately want to jump into the realm of worship, prayer and music; especially when they know the ramifications of their actions and activities.

This is why Streaming in Heaven's Flow has such meaning and power on it. If we see a model from Heaven's realm, and it is full of anointing and bearing fruit, how much more should we enter into the same actions. The Word of God will endure forever.

Isaiah 40:8

> *The grass is withered, and the flower is fallen:*
> *but the word of our Lord **endures for ever**.* (RHE)
>
> *"The grass withers, the flowers fade, but the word of our God **remains** forever."* (HCS)
>
> *"Grass dies and wildflowers fall. But the word of our God **continues** forever."* (ERV)
>
> *The grass, hath withered, the flower, hath faded, -*
> *but the word of our God, shall stand unto times age-abiding!* (REB)

As this power in the Word of God comes forth [singing it and praying it] it now becomes **transforming power** that changes the spiritual atmosphere and the condition of our hearts.

Study, Discuss and Think About:

❖ There is a great need for people to know the Bible. They need to have the Word of God deeply planted in their hearts. The book of Romans records that faith comes by hearing and hearing by the Word of God. How would you implement the singing and memorization of the Word of God for your life, your church and your friends?

❖ Let the teaching of Christ and His words keep on liv_____ in you. Keep on teaching and helping each other. Sing the Songs of Da_____ and the church songs and the songs of Hea_____ with hearts full of thanks to God.

❖ Concerning holy songs of praise and songs of the Spirit: why is it important that singers and musicians understand these two realms?

The High Praises of God in Our Mouth
The Two-Edged Sword in Our Hand

The Warfare Psalm, Psalm 149 is about the ability of God's weapons. This is the honor for all His godly ones: the power of worship and prayer releases justice and judgment.

1. Anointed Prayer and Worship Releases God's Justice

Psalm 149:5 - 9

⁵ Let the godly ones exalt in glory; let them **sing** for joy **on** their **beds**.
⁶ Let the **high praises** of God be in their mouth, and a **two-edged sword** in their hand,

⁷ To execute vengeance on the nations, and punishment on the peoples.
⁸ To bind their kings with chains, and their nobles with fetters of iron,
⁹ To execute on them **the judgment** written;
this is an honor for all His godly ones. Praise the LORD!

It begins for me with the power of a human voice to utter words that ride on wonderful melodies. These words and melodies affect both the hearer and the spiritual realm into which they are released. We have so much music and so many songs flooding by us in our average day that we have grown used to the impact of even the simplest song.

2. For the Lord Loves Justice

We are becoming God's people of prayer, worship and justice. Most believers have been a part of worship and some kind of prayer. But most have never been taught about the Lord's justice. We have been raised up like Queen Esther for **such a time as this**:

to sing, to pray out the judgment and justice of God on the earth as worshipping intercessors.

Psalm 37:28 - 30 The Mouth of the Righteous Tongue Speaks Justice

²⁸ For the LORD **loves justice** and does not forsake His godly ones; they are preserved forever, but the descendants of the wicked will be **cut off**.

²⁹ The righteous will inherit the land and dwell in it forever.

³⁰ The mouth of the righteous utters wisdom, and **his tongue speaks justice**.

Psalm 33:4 - 5 The Lord Loves Mercy and Justice

⁴ For the word of the LORD is upright and all His work is done in faithfulness.
⁵ **He loves** righteousness and **justice**; The earth is full of the lovingkindness of the LORD.

He loves whatever is **just** and **good**, and His unfailing love fills the earth.
He loves **mercy** and **judgment**; the earth is full of the mercy of the Lord.

It is super important that you begin to study justice right now. Justice is the key to understanding the love of God. I know it seems that the opposite is true. But true love operates with the spirit of justice working in love. Justice without the power of God's love is limited in changing the heart of human beings.

3. Two-Edged Sword in Our Hands

Let the high praises of God be in their mouth, in a holy zeal for His honor, let them take a two-edged sword in their hand, to fight His battles against the enemies of His kingdom.

(Matthew Henry Commentary)

Psalm 144:1 goes hand in hand with Psalm 149:6. They both speak of the warfare theme and of what God has put in our hands. I have always viewed my voice, my guitar, my hands and my piano as extensions of my life and heart. Further, I see them as consecrated, dedicated weapons made ready for God's use.

Psalm 144:1 - *Blessed be the LORD, my rock,*
Who trains my hands for war, and my fingers for battle.

Psalm 149:6 - *Let the **high praises** of God be in their mouth,*
*a **two-edged sword** in their hand.*

A. When We are Singing and Praying the Word of God, the written Word is judgment in and of itself. It is enough to overpower evil and triumph over darkness.

B. Passionate Prayer Opens Spiritual Gateways ascending into Heaven. The depths of worship is a tool and weapon of priesthood that flows with spiritual might on it.

 Revelations and Thoughts: _____

4. Anointed Prayer and Worship Releases God's Justice

A. Measuring out the Judgment and Justice of God

Jesus said, *"...The ruler of this world has been judged."*

John 16:7 - 11 *But I tell you the truth, it is to your advantage that I go away; for if I do not go away, the Helper will not come to you; but if I go, I will send Him to you.*

*And He when He comes, will convict the world concerning sin and righteousness and **judgment**;*

1. concerning sin, because they do not believe in Me; and

2. concerning righteousness, because I go to the Father and you no longer see Me; and

*3. concerning judgment, because **the ruler of this world has been judged**.*

This is truly a powerful point that Jesus left with us for our good and His Kingdom's release.

*Now judgment is upon **this world**; now the ruler of this world will be cast out . . . John 12:31 About judgment, because the ruler (evil genius, prince) of this world [Satan] is judged and condemned and sentence already is passed upon him.* John 16:11 (AMP)

So here's the point, as we are praying and worshipping, we are releasing the justice of God and the judgment of the Lord already written and passed upon the devil himself.

Remember: satan is a fallen angel. He is not and never will be even close to the power and the place of Jesus as the Son of God. One of our commissions in spiritual warfare is to sing and pray the Word of God to where it begins to confuse and bind the kingdom of darkness.

B. Taking Our Place as Warring Worshippers

We have a role with our prayers, our music and our intercessions to help release the judgments that have already been written by the Lord Himself against the kingdom of darkness.

Realms of God's power and light are released
as we are doing prayer and flowing in worship.

We give all the glory to the Lord for this manifestation for we know that it is generated by the anointing of His Holy Spirit. We approach these things will all humility but we take our place as **warring worshippers**.

 Revelations and Thoughts: _____

5. The Authority of the Crucified Lamb and Victorious Lion

With Jesus, real authority comes from three distinct realms.
One: Who He is as the King of Glory.
Two: What He has done as the Crucified Lamb of God.
Three: His place in Heaven and His return as the Victorious Lion.

Matthew 28 : 16 - 18

[16] *But the eleven disciples proceeded to Galilee, to the mountain which Jesus had designated.*
[17] *When they saw Him, **they worshiped Him**; but some were doubtful.*

[18] *And Jesus came up and spoke to them, saying,*
*   **All authority** has been given to Me in heaven and on earth.*

Our inheritance is to take our place in Him with His authority to do intercession full of blessing and spiritual warfare. His presence and Lordship gives us real power on earth and in the spiritual realm. We need to pray for a genuine revelation for worship teams and believers all over the world to understand this.

This is the time to be found Streaming in Heaven's Flow using His anointing on your praise and worship to bring Him glory and conquer evil. Don't stop what you know to be right and powerful. Do it even more until His Kingdom comes and His will is done.

 Revelations and Thoughts: _____

6. The Power of the Simplest Songs

Consider the power of the human voice to utter words that ride on wonderful melodies; these words and melodies effect both the hearer and the spiritual realm to which they are released. When you go back through human history, you'll find the simplest songs are **life changing**, **load bearing** and have the power to carry the human soul through the darkest of hours.

A. **Negro Spirituals are Christian Songs**, most of them concern what the Bible says and how to live with (in) the Spirit of God. These songs carried the African slaves through the length and breadth of one of the darkest hours of human history.

B. **The High Praises of God**

The high praises of God were simple songs that the Hebrew people sang. They are full of what we now know as the canonized Word of God. Simple word phrases were put to simple melodies. People from denominational backgrounds during the Charismatic Renewal learned the Word of God more in depth because as they sang scripture songs. It was a worship, song movement that went around the world in less than 20 years.

Revelations and Thoughts: _____

_____

_____

Study, Discuss and Think About:

❖ How wonderful is it to know that the high praises of God in your mouth and the Word of God coming from your heart has the power of Heaven standing behind it? Explain why your words and melodies are important both to the Lord and in this world.

❖ From Psalm 37:28-30 for the L_____ loves jus_____ and does not forsake His godly one. The mouth of the righ_____ utters wisdom and his ton_____ speaks justice.

❖ With Jesus, real authority comes from three distinct realms.
    One: Who He is as the _____ of _____.
    Two: What He has done as the _____ _____ of God.
    Three: His place in Heaven and His return as the _____ _____.

Urgency! Take Heed, Watch and Pray

Be circumspect, (looking), praying and be devout.
Because you don't know when the Lord will be returning.

Mark 13:32 - 37 No One Knows the Day or the Hour

^{32} *"But of that day and hour no one knows, not even the angels in heaven,*
nor the Son, but only the Father.

^{33} ***Take heed, watch and pray;*** *for you do not know when the time is.*
Be on your guard [constantly alert], and watch and pray;
for you do not know when the time will come.   (AMP)
Be ***circumspect****, be* ***vigilant****, and* ***devout****:*
because you are uncertain when that time will be.   (MNT)

^{34} *It is like a man going to a far country, who left his house and gave authority to his servants,*
and to each his work, and commanded the doorkeeper to watch.

^{35} ***Watch therefore, for you do not know when the master of the house is coming --***
in the evening, at midnight, at the crowing of the rooster, or in the morning,

^{36} *lest, coming suddenly, he find you sleeping.*
^{37} *And what I say to you,* ***I say to all: Watch!"***

In the gospel of Mark, the thirteenth chapter, there is a tremendous unfolding of revelation on the elements of the sign of the times and the end of the age. When will these things happen and what are the signs?   (Mark 13:1 - 5)

The importance of prayer, **staying alert** (which is in every believer's ability to do daily) and the power of seeing is magnified in light of Jesus' words. **Take heed, watch and pray!!** These three things keep us in fresh oil and on track so we can be prepared (ready) for the time that is coming and even more so His second coming. Now let's define each one of these.

Revelations and Thoughts: _____

_____

_____

1. Take Heed

Take heed, starts for me with a military and police term "your head should be on a swivel." It is referring to walking about with 360 degree vision and sensitivity. I am amazed with the number of people who are caught off guard many times a week by things that are taking place around them. They haven't even noticed them. In other words, they don't know **what** is going on around them.

The phrase, "**take heed**" is defined like this - these are more about the natural eye:

* to see, discern, as with the bodily eye; to use the **power** of **seeing**;
* to **turn the eyes** to anything; to look at or upon, gaze at

These are more about spiritual or mentally seeing:

* to have understanding; to discern mentally, perceive, **discover**
* to consider, contemplate, to weigh carefully, examine

Active prayer and intercession opens and increases the realm of our seeing and makes available higher grade spiritual vision. There is one other dimension of taking heed that is really powerful. In a geographical sense of places, mountains, buildings, etc. it means **turning towards** any quarter or facing it.

Prayer and devotion give us a greater ability to "turn toward any quarter." We can face things head on in prayer and worship that otherwise we may avoid or run away from. This is why a greater dedication to prayer is so important.

2. Watch

Watch should be more readily understood by each one us. If you drive a car, if you ride a bike, or if you go running in the morning or evening, you had better be watching. If not, an accident is sure to happen.

The phrase "**to watch**" is defined - these are more about staying awake and being attentive:

* to keep awake, attentive, ready; to be circumspect, prudent, **guarded**
* to exercise constant vigilance over something
    [drawn from the image of the (good) shepherd]

These are more about alertness:

* a wakeful frame of mind, as opposed to listlessness
* signifies the state untouched by slumber, or beclouding influences

These definitions can be used in all of our prayer times. Right now in our Prayer Room, one of the major topics we are praying about is "Awakening." If we are watching, we will be able to discern the current sleeping state of the Church. We will feel the need to intercede for our own awakening and the church itself.

The whole element of "watching" opens the door for us to start moving into greater awakening. Literally, these definitions should work their way into our vocabulary for prayer. We should mark this in our memory, that our prayers are rising like incense before the Lord. Our prayers, worship and intercession is effecting change both in time and in the spirit dimension.

Revelations and Thoughts: _____

_____

Ephesians 5:14 - *For this reason He says, **"Awake, sleeper,***
*and arise from the dead, and Christ will **shine on you."***

Therefore He says, Awake, O sleeper. Up! thou sleeper,
*wake up from your sleep, **climb out of your coffins;***
Christ shall shine (make day dawn) upon you and give you (show) you light. (MSG)

3. Pray - The phrase "**to pray**" is defined like this:

This is as simple as talking to the Lord. Most prayer is offered in faith because you believe that God is bigger than your situation or the things that you are praying over and about.

Pray - be devout - to throw or to **pour forth words** or sounds; to pour out prayers

- ❖ to bless . . . to preach . . . to intercede . . . to intervene
- ❖ to pour forth water, as in a violent rain
- ❖ to supplicate good : (entreat or urge)
- ❖ to ask with earnestness or zeal, as for a favor or something desirable

Prayer within worship means to supplicate, implore; to ask with true reverence and humility.

Devout - yielding a **reverential attention** to God;
with ardent (heart-felt) devotion to the Lord

4. Four Prayer Principles

There are four prayer principles found in Mark 13. Each one is full of God's provision and saving grace.

First truth - Prayer brings light and illumination.

Second truth - Do not be troubled, only have a pray-full spirit.

Third truth - Take heed, watch and pray.

Fourth truth - Jesus' counsel in light of it all, "I say to all: Watch!"

Jesus said we must do this, the "take heed, watch and pray" lifestyle. This command covers the whole of the Body of Christ. Everyone should be in a place where they are on their guard (AMP). We are going to be watching, on the alert (NAS) wakeful and praying (GLT). Let's get busy doing what Jesus said.

Mark 13:32 - 34

> [32] *But of that day and hour no one knows, not even the angels*
> *in heaven, nor the Son, but only the Father.*
> [33] ***Take heed, watch and pray;***
> *for you do not know when the time is.*
> [34] *It is like a man going to a far country, who left his house and **gave authority** to his servants,*
> *and to each his work, and commanded the doorkeeper to watch.*

Revelations and Thoughts: _____

_____

Study, Discuss and Think About:

❖ TAKE HEED defined in military and police terms goes like this, "your head should be on a swivel." It is referring to walking around with _____ degree vision and sensitivity. So how would you change your lifestyle to be more on guard and sensitive the Spirit and peoples needs around you?

❖ WATCH: The element of "watching" opens the door for us to what? _____ Because our prayers, worship and intercession affect change in what two dimensions?

❖ PRAY: Review the four prayer principles found in Mark 13 and write down which one is most important to you and why?

God Trains Our Hands for War
and Our Fingers for Battle

BLESSED BE the Lord, my Rock and my keen and firm strength,
    Who (trains) teaches my hands for war and my fingers for battle.

1. It Was the Lord Who Trained David's Hands for War

Psalm 144:1 - *Blessed be the LORD, my rock,*
    *Who **trains my hands for war**, and my **fingers** for **battle**;*

BLESSED BE the Lord, my Rock and my keen and firm Strength,
    Who teaches my hands to war and my fingers to fight. (AMP)

*. . . teaching my hands **the use** of the sword, and my fingers **the art** of fighting:* (BBE)

He gives me strength for war and skill for battle. (NLT)

David trained God's people too, for as he was the sweet singer of Israel, so he was the captain of their hosts, and taught the children of Judah the use of the bow and taught their hands to war, as God had taught his.   (Matthew Henry Commentary)

Psalm 18:33 - 34   Trains My Hands For Battle

[33] *He makes my feet like hinds' feet, and sets me upon my high places.*
[34] *He **trains my hands for battle**, so that my arms can bend a bow of bronze.*

2. Warring Worshippers

As you do spiritual warfare with **God's holy power**, the judgment that has already been written by the hand of God is being executed against the kingdom of darkness. As you let the high praises of God stay in your mouth and release the power of the two-edged sword in your hand, you become a **warring worshipper**.

Worship is a weapon [His Presence] - Enemies destroy themselves while Judah worshipped.

2 Chronicles 20:20 - 25

[20] *. . .Jehoshaphat stood and said, "Listen to me, O Judah and inhabitants of Jerusalem, put your trust in the LORD your God and you will be established. Put your trust in His prophets and succeed."*

[21] *When he had consulted with the people, he appointed those who sang to the LORD and those who praised Him in holy attire, as they went out before the army and said,*
    "Give thanks to the LORD, for His lovingkindness is everlasting."

[22] *When they began **singing** and **praising**, the LORD set ambushes against the sons of Ammon, Moab and Mount Seir, who had come against Judah; so they were routed.*

23 *For the sons of Ammon and Moab rose up against (those) of Mount Seir destroying them completely; when they had finished with the inhabitants of Seir, they helped to destroy one another.*

24 *When Judah came to the lookout of the wilderness, they looked toward the multitude, and behold, they were corpses lying on the ground, and no one had escaped.*

25 *When Jehoshaphat and his people came to take their spoil, they found much among them, including goods, garments and valuable things which they took for themselves, more than they could carry.*
And they were three days taking the spoil because there was so much.

Revelations and Thoughts: _____

_____

_____

3. Understanding Your Place as a Musical or Vocal Spiritual Warrior

The principles found in Psalm 149 help you understand spiritual warfare. Real worship and prayer released at their highest levels, begin to inhibit and interfere with the dominion of the demonic kingdom. It will blast holes right through the blanket of spiritual oppression set up by the kingdom of darkness.

The effect of true worship and intercession . . .
blesses the heart of God and terrorizes the kingdom of darkness.

Psalm 149 : 9 - *Let the high praises of God be in their mouths and two-edged swords in their hands,*

*1. to **execute** vengeance on the nations*

2. and chastisement on the people,

3. to bind their kings with chains and their nobles with fetters of iron,

4. to execute on them the judgment written! This is glory for all His faithful ones. Hallelujah! (RSV, BER)

4. Jesus has Disarmed the Rulers and Principalities

Colossians 2 : 3 -15

13 *When you were dead in your transgressions and the uncircumcision of your flesh, He made you alive together with Him, having forgiven us all our transgressions,*

14 *having canceled out the certificate of debt consisting of decrees against us, which was hostile to us; and He has taken it out of the way, having nailed it to the cross.*

15 *When He had **disarmed the rulers and authorities,** He made a (bold) public display of them, having **triumphed over them** through Him.* (NAS)

15 *He disarmed, **spoiled the principalities and powers** that were ranged against us . .* (KJV)

I am so very grateful for the power of the life of the Crucified Lamb of God as our Risen Savior. We must continue to rejoice in the fact that He disarmed the rulers and authorities of the kingdom of darkness. So our leading worship, singing and playing is done off of this platform of His great work because of the Cross. We become part of the public display of His triumphing over them every time we choose to worship and release His presence.

Revelations and Thoughts: _____

Study, Discuss, Think About:

❖ Why would there be a need for the Lord to train our hands for war and our fingers for battle? Don't overlook the obvious in answering this question. All of us have ene_____.

❖ If you had a choice to be a "worshipping warrior" or a "warring worshipper," which would you choose and why?

(Remember the adjective comes first, because it describes the noun.
But the noun declares the subject. So when the describer goes away, what are you?)

❖ According to Colossians 2, Jesus has disa_____ the ru_____ and

aut_____. He made a bold public display of them, having tri_____ over

them. He spo_____ the principalities and powers that were ranged (arranged) against us.

Anointed Prayer and Worship Release God's Justice

1. Measuring Out the Judgment and Justice of God

Jesus said, " . . .The ruler of this world has been judged."

> **John 16:7-11** - *But I tell you the truth, it is to your advantage that I go away; for if I do not go away, the Helper will not come to you; but if I go, I will send Him to you.*
>
> *And He, when He comes, will convict the world concerning sin and righteousness and **judgment**;*
>
> > *1. concerning sin, because they do not believe in Me; and*
> >
> > *2. concerning righteousness, because I go to the Father and you no longer see Me;*
> >
> > *3. concerning judgment, because **the ruler of this world has been judged**.*

A. Jesus Said, "If I am lifted up from the earth." Both on the Cross and through the Gospel

> **John 12:31-32** *"Now judgment is upon this world; now the ruler of this world will be cast out. And I, if I am lifted up from the earth, will draw all men to Myself."*

We are the servants of the Lord who stand as prophetic worshipping intercessors. As we pray, we release the stored up, transforming power of His Word. We have the honor, as friends of the Bridegroom, to help establish His Kingdom's coming and seeing thousands turn to the Lord as the darkness comes off of them.

When we intercede, we become "a **mouthpiece** of the Lord." We are on the earth doing His bidding and the "judgments written" are being released and enforced.

B. For Such A Time As This: God's People of Prayer, Worship and Justice

We have been raised up like Queen Esther for **such a time as this**: to sing and pray out the judgments and justice of God on the earth as worshipping intercessors.

2. The Lord Loves Justice

> **Psalm 37:28-30**
>
> [28] *For the LORD **loves justice** and does not forsake His godly ones; they are preserved forever, but the descendants of the wicked will be **cut off**.*
>
> [29] *The righteous will inherit the land and dwell in it forever.*
>
> [30] *The mouth of the righteous utters wisdom, and **his tongue speaks justice**.*
>
> **Psalm 33:4-5** The Lord Loves Mercy and Justice
>
> [4] *For the word of the LORD is upright and all His work is done in faithfulness.*
>
> [5] ***He loves** righteousness and **justice**; The earth is full of the lovingkindness of the LORD.*
>
> *He loves whatever is **just** and **good**, and His unfailing love fills the earth. He loves **mercy** and **judgment**; the earth is full of the mercy of the Lord*

Very clearly, the Lord Himself loves justice. Whatever is just and good, whatever is full of mercy and justice, the Lord loves these things. Let's join with the heart of God and love the things He loves and hate the things He hates. I know it sounds way over the top, but it is actually part of the Word of God.

Proverbs 6:16 - 19

[16]*These six things the LORD hates, Yes, seven are an abomination to Him:*
[17]*A proud look, a lying tongue, hands that shed innocent blood,*
[18]*A heart that devises wicked plans, feet that are swift in running to evil,*
[19]*A false witness who speaks lies, and one who sows discord among brethren.*

3. God Will Not Pervert Justice - He does not act wickedly

A. Doing Righteousness and Justice

Doing is a verb. It is an action word, not a passive noun. We should join our heart to that which is the same in the heart of our Heavenly Father. I have had a strong sense of justice all my life. I hate prejudice in all of its forms, social, financial, skin color, etc. Through our prayer and worship, we can begin to destroy the perversion of justice.

Job 34:12 - *Surely, God will not act wickedly, and the Almighty will not **pervert justice**.*

Job 8:3 - *Does God pervert justice? Or does the Almighty **pervert** what is right?*

Genesis 18:19

*"For I have chosen him [Abraham], so that he may command his children and his household after him to keep the way of the LORD by **doing righteousness** and **justice**, so that the LORD may bring upon Abraham what He has spoken about him."*

Exodus 23:2

*"You shall not follow the masses in doing evil, nor shall you testify in a dispute so as to turn aside after a multitude in order to **pervert justice**;"*

B. Righteousness and Justice are the Foundation of His Throne

God by His very nature cannot pervert justice. It is against the make-up of His whole being concerning good and what is morally right. The Scripture records that even His Throne is established on righteousness and justice.

Psalm 89:14 - 15
Righteousness and justice are the foundation of Your throne; lovingkindness and truth go before You. How blessed are the people who know the joyful sound!
O LORD, they walk in the light of Your countenance.

Here simply defined is the Hebrew language definition of to pervert or corrupt.

pervert - to cause to turn aside or away from what is good or true or morally right
corrupt - to cause to turn aside or away from what is generally done or accepted

misdirect - a. to divert to a wrong end or purpose: **misuse**
b. to twist the meaning or sense of: **misinterpret**

Synonyms: to bend, color, cook, distort; falsify, fudge, misinterpret, misrelate, misrepresent, misstate, garble, slant, twist, warp

 Revelations and Thoughts: _____

_____

4. We are Empowered Through Our Union with a Holy God

Ephesians 6:10 - 11 Be Strong: Fighting with the Strength of His Might

¹⁰ *Finally, be strong in the Lord and in the strength of His might . . . [be **empowered through your union with Him**]; and that strength which His boundless might provides.* (AMP)

*. . . draw your strength from the Lord, the Mastery which **His conquering power** supplies*
(CON, KNOX)

1. Empowered by Him: We are seated in Heavenly places with Christ Jesus.

2. His might is boundless: This is why we do prayer and worship in His strength.

3. He holds conquering power: He rides on in Victory!

> **Psalm 45: 3 - 4**
> ³ Gird Your sword on *Your* thigh, O Mighty One, *in* Your splendor and
> Your majesty! ⁴ And in Your majesty **ride on victoriously**,
> for the cause of truth and meekness *and* righteousness;
> let Your right hand teach You awesome things.

B. With Well-made Weapons: We Stand against the Schemes of the devil - (Eph. 6:11)

¹¹ *Put on God's whole armor [the armor of **a heavy-armed soldier** which God supplies], that you may be able successfully to stand up against [all] the strategies and the deceits of the devil.* (AMP)

*So take everything the Master has set out for you, **well-made weapons** of the best materials. And **put them to use** so you will be able to stand up to everything the devil throws your way.* (MSG)

*You must **wear all the weapons** in God's armory.* (KNOX)

1. Take it up and put it on

2. Armor supplied by God

3. God's wisdom and armor is greater

 Revelations and Thoughts: _____

_____

5. Three Super Anointed Heavenly Elements: Worship, Prayer and Music

Our battle on the earth is not against flesh and blood. It is against the spiritual forces of wickedness. The Lord provided a triple threat anointing for us to use in victory.

Ephesians 6: 12 - *For our struggle [fight] is not against flesh and blood, but* (NAS, Phi)

❖ *against **principalities** (the rulers, despotisms, that is tyranny [ies]),*

❖ *against the powers (**authorities** of darkness),* (NLT, YLT) *[like territorial gate keepers]*

❖ *against the world forces, the various powers of evil in this darkness,* (TCNT)
    *against [the **master spirits** who are] the world rulers of **this present darkness**,*

❖ *the spiritual **forces of wickedness** in high places, in supernatural sphere(s)* (KJV, AMP)
    The spiritual agents of evil arrayed against us in the heavenly warfare (Wey, Phi)

Worship . . . Prayer . . . Music: Heaven's triple - threat anointing triumphs over darkness!!

Using invisible weapons against invisible forces:

the Word of God sang or prayed out loud (invisible)
anointed music from consecrated hearts (invisible)
your worship and intercession invisible to the natural eye

Let Us Forever Make the Connection

When we are doing our music, worship and intercession, there is an inherent "God power" released in it that is a true form of spiritual warfare. It blesses and helps real people while thwarting the activities of the kingdom of darkness.

Revelations and Thoughts: _____

_____

Study, Discuss and Think About:

❖ We are the servants of the Lord who stand as prophetic worshipping int_____.
As we pray, we release the stored up, transforming power of His Word. We have the ho____, as friends of the Br_____, to help establish His Kingdom's coming and seeing thousands turn to the Lord as the da_____ comes off of them.

❖ Why is it important that we pray the Word concerning justice and judgment?
Think of this question in light of Psalm 37's declarations:

(a) "the Lord loves justice and   (b) the tongue of the righteous speaks justice."

❖ We have powerful resources and weapons in the Lord. Ephesians 6:11

*Put on God's whole armor [the armor of **a heavy-armed soldier** which God supplies], that you may be able successfully to stand up against [all] the strategies and the deceits of the devil.*

List the two most important and powerful elements in this verse.

1. _____

2. _____

Ephesians 5: 14 - 21   Awake O Sleeper and Redeem the Time

Section 1: Prayer for True Awakening in Our Region, Nation and Churches

[14] Therefore He says, "**Awake, O sleeper**, and arise from the dead.
  Wake up from your sleep, **climb out of your coffins**;
  Christ will show you the light!
      Christ shall (make day dawn) upon you and give you light
      and where your light shines, it will expose their evil deeds.

[15] Therefore be careful how you walk, not as unwise men (fools) but as wise.
  Look carefully then how you walk! **Live purposefully** and worthily and accurately,
      not as the unwise and witless, but as wise people,

[16] making the most of your time, because the days are evil. **Redeeming the time**, for the days are evil. Make the most of every opportunity for doing good. These are desperate times!

> **Now Offer Your Prayer:**

Section 2: Prayer for Light and Understanding of the Will of God

[17] So then do not be foolish, but **understand what the will of the Lord is**.
  Therefore do not be vague and thoughtless, but understanding and firmly grasping what the will of the Lord is. **Don't act carelessly**, but try to understand
              what the Lord wants you to do, what the Master wants.

[18] And do not get drunk with wine, for that is dissipation, **but be ever filled** with the [Holy] Spirit.
  Don't be drunk with wine, because that will ruin your life.
          Instead, **let the Holy Spirit fill and control you**.

> **Now Offer Your Prayer:**

Section 3: Prayer for the Greater Release of Worship and the Spirit of Thanksgiving

[19] speaking to one another in **psalms** and **hymns** and **spiritual songs**,
          singing and making melody with your heart to the Lord; **offering praise** with
  voices [instruments], making melody with all your heart to the Lord,

      . . . music to the Lord in your hearts. **Sing songs from your heart** to Christ.

[20] **always giving thanks** for all things, at all times and for everything
          giving thanks in the name of our Lord Jesus Christ to God the Father.
      Sing praises over everything, any excuse for a song to God the Father
          in the name of our Master, Jesus Christ.

[21] and be subject to one another **in the fear of Christ**.   **Be subject** to one another out of reverence for Christ (the Messiah, the Anointed One)
      Out of respect for Christ, be courteously reverent to one another.

> **Now Offer Your Prayer:**

Psalm 82: 1 - 5, 8   The Psalm of Justice [Asaph]

Section 1: Pray for justice and its eminent and abundant release. Hallelujah!!

¹ God takes His stand in His own congregation; **He judges** in the midst of the rulers.
    God presides over heaven's court; **He pronounces judgment** on the judges:
    God calls the judges into His courtroom; He puts all the judges in the dock (et).

² How long will you **judge unjustly** and **show partiality** to the wicked?   Selah.
    How long will you judges hand down unjust decisions?
    How long will you shower special favors on the wicked?
    How long will you **judge perversely** and the countenances of the lawless, (be) uplifted?

Now Offer Your Prayer:

Section 2: True Justice for the Weak and the Fatherless, Vindicate the Poor and the Orphan

³ **Vindicate:** the **weak** and **fatherless**; **Do justice:** to the **afflicted** and **destitute**.

    "Give **fair judgment:** to the **poor** and the **orphan**;
        Uphold the rights: of the **oppressed** and the **destitute**.

You're here to **defend the defenseless**, to make sure that underdogs get a fair break;

    Judge for the **needy** and **fatherless**: **do justice** to the **humble** and the **poor**."

⁴ "**Rescue** the **weak** and **needy**; deliver *them* out of the hand of the wicked.
        Rescue the **poor** and **helpless**; deliver them from the grasp of evil people.

    [You judges] your job is to **stand up for the powerless**,
                                and prosecute all those who exploit them."

Now Offer Your Prayer:

Section 3: Prayer for the True Administration of Justice in Our Legal System

⁵ They [the magistrates and judges] do not know - nor do they understand;
    (Ignorant judges! Head-in-the-sand judges! They haven't a clue to what's going on.)

        they walk about in darkness [complacent satisfaction];
        all the foundations of the earth are shaken [to the core].

    [The fundamental principles upon which rests **the administration of justice.**]

⁸ **Arise, O God,** judge the earth! . . . for to You belong all the nations.
    Rise, O God, judge the earth,   . . . for Thou hast inheritance among all the nations!
                . . . for it is You who possesses all the nations.

O God, give them their just deserts! **You've got the whole world in Your hands!**

Now Offer Your Prayer:

Ephesians 1: 15 -23   The Spirit of Wisdom and Revelation

Section 1: Father, Grow Our Prayer Lives and Our Ability to Focus on You

[15] For this reason, because I have heard of your faith in the Lord Jesus [the solid trust you have in the Master] and your love toward all the saints (the people of God),   [MSG]

[16] I do not cease to give thanks for you, (while) **making mention of you in my prayers**.

. . . and I never give up praying for you   (Phi)

Now Offer Your Prayer:

Section 2: Lord, Grant Us Greater Revelation, Open the Eyes of Our Heart

[17] [For I pray to] the God of our Lord Jesus Christ, the Father of glory,
that He may **grant you a spirit of wisdom and revelation**
[insight into mysteries and secrets] in the [deep and intimate] knowledge of Him,

[18] (praying that **the eyes of your heart may be enlightened**)
by having your heart **flooded with light**, so that you can know and understand (the hope of His calling) and how rich is His glorious inheritance in the saints (His set-apart ones),

[19] And [so that you can **know**] **the unlimited and surpassing greatness of His power** in us who believe, as demonstrated in the working of (the strength of His might).

Now Offer Your Prayer:

Section 3: Praying the Great Authority and Dominion of Christ on the Earth

[20] Which He exerted (accomplished) in Christ when He raised Him from the dead and seated Him at His [own] right hand in the heavenly [places],   (RSV)

[21] **Far above** all rule and [government] . . . **Far above** all authority and power . . .
Far above (every principality) and dominion . . . and even every name that is named,
not only in this age and in this world,
but also in the age and the world which are to come.   (KJV) [WNT]

[22] And He has subjected **all things** (under the power of Christ), **underneath His feet** and has appointed Him the Head (over all things) for at the center of all this,
Christ rules the church.   (Phi)

[23] Which is His body, the fullness of Him **Who fills all in all,** making them complete,
and Who fills everything **everywhere with Himself**.

Now Offer Your Prayer:

Psalm 144:1 - 2, 9 - 15   Blessed be The Lord My Rock and Firm Strength

Section 1: You Train My Hands for War and My Fingers for Battle

¹ BLESSED be the Lord, my **Rock** and firm **Strength**, Who trains my hands for **war** and
my fingers to **fight** - -   You give me strength for war and skill for battle.

² My loving **Ally** and my **Fortress**, my **High Tower** of Safety and my Deliverer, You stand before
me as a **Shield** and in Whom I trust and take **refuge**, who subdues nations under me.

You are the **bedrock** on which I stand, the **castle** in which I live, my **rescuing knight**,
The **high crag** where I run for dear life, while he lays my enemies low.

Now Offer Your Prayer:

Section 2: Sing a New Song to the God of Your Salvation

⁹ I will sing **a new song** to You, O God; upon a harp of ten strings I will **sing praises** to You,

¹⁰ You are He who **gives salvation** to kings, who rescues David His servant from the evil sword.
For you grant **victory** to kings! You are the one who rescued your servant David.

¹¹ Save me from the fatal sword! Rescue me from the power of my enemies.
Their mouths are full of lies; they swear to tell the truth, but they lie.

Now Offer Your Prayer:

Section 3: Bless Our Sons and Daughters, Bless Us with Your Increase and Protection

¹² Let our **sons** in their youth be as plants grown large and
our **daughters** as sculptured corner pillars hewn like those of a palace;
may our sons flourish in their youth like well-nurtured plants.
May our daughters be like **graceful pillars**, carved to beautify a palace.

¹³ Let our garners (barns, our farms) **be full**, furnishing every kind of produce, a*nd* our flocks
bring forth thousands and ten thousands in our fields; fill our barns with great harvest

¹⁴ Let our cattle bear without mishap and without loss, when there is no invasion
[of hostile armies] and no going forth [against besiegers!]
May there be no breached walls, no forced exile, no cries of distress in our squares.
Protect us from invasion and exile -- eliminate the crime in our streets.

¹⁵ How **blessed are the people** who are so situated;
How blessed are the people **whose God is the LORD!**

Now Offer Your Prayer:

Psalm 29:3 - 9   The Voice of the Lord is Thundering - It's the "Psalm of Seven Thunders!"

Section 1: The Voice of the Lord – Truly Awesome, Excellent and Formidable

[3] The voice of the LORD, (the Eternal) is upon the waters; (peels across the waters)

> It is the God of glory (of shining greatness) thundering, across (over) the waters (NLB)
> God, Brilliant, His voice and His face, streaming brightness roars out over the vast deeps.
> (Mof., Har., REB)   The LORD thunders (fulminates - shouts forth decrees) over the mighty sea.
> GOD, across the flood waters.

[4] The voice of the Lord is powerful, mighty in operation), it is resplendent with power.   (PBV, Har.)

The voice of the LORD is majestic, the voice of the Lord has a noble sound.   (BBE)   The voice of
Yahweh, is with power,   GOD's thunder tympanic (tympani drums),   GOD's thunder symphonic.

[5] The voice of the LORD breaks (splits) the mighty cedars;

> His voice is breaking them into pieces even uprooting (shatters) the cedars of Lebanon. (Har., ASV)

Now Offer Your Prayer:

Section 2: The Voice of the Lord carves out tongues of fire

[6] He makes Lebanon skip like a calf, and Sirion like a young wild ox.

This voice makes Lebanon and Sirion like the bull-calves of wild oxen.

> They spring forth like a young antelope (leaping and dancing).   (Rhm, DeW.)

[7] The voice of the LORD hews out flames of fire, carves out tongues of flashing fire.

> The voice of the Lord splits and flashes forth forked lightning, strikes with lightning bolts.
> The voice of Yahweh, is cleaving out flames of fire;
> (flashes forth) sharpening lightening shafts.   (Har. Jerus.)

Now Offer Your Prayer:

Section 3: The voice of the LORD makes the deer to calve and strips the forests bare;

[8] The voice of the LORD shakes the wilderness; (makes the desert tremble and quake)

> This voice brings birth pains among the wilderness, writhing in travail, the sand whirls,
> the desert trembles even the large wilderness of Kadesh.   (Rhm, Mof., Har.)

[9] The voice of the LORD makes the deer to calve and strips the forests bare;

> The voice of the Lord makes the hinds bring forth their young, the voice of the LORD twists
> mighty oaks. and twists down the trees, into toothpicks (PBV)

> And in His temple everything says, "Glory!" while in His temple everyone is saying, Glory!
> In his Temple everyone shouts, "Glory!" While in His palace all are chanting, "Glory! Glory!"

> Meanwhile, in His sanctuary, there is **no sound** but tells of His glory. Surely, through this,
> His universal temple, everything speaks of His glory. (Mof., KNOX, Sprl.)

Now Offer Your Prayer:

1 Chronicles 4:10 - The Prayer of Jabez

Section 1: It is Your Desire Lord to Bless, Enlarge, Give Favor and Keep Us From Evil

Now **Jabez** called on the God of Israel, he cried (out) , saying,
"Oh that You would   1) **bless** me (Lord) <u>indeed</u> and
2) **enlarge** my territories (borders) , and
that Your hand of   3) **favor** would be **with me**, and
that You would   4) **keep** me from (**evil**) harm, that I may not cause pain!!"
So God granted him what he requested.   (NAS, AMP. NKJV)

And Jabez called upon the God of Israel, saying: If blessing Thou will bless me,
and will enlarge my borders, and Thy hand be with me, and Thou save me from **being oppressed by evil**. And God granted him the things he prayed for.   (RHE)

Now Offer Your Prayer:

Section 2: The Blessing of the Lord Does Make Rich

Proverbs 10:22 - It is the **blessing** of the LORD that makes rich, And He adds no sorrow to it.

Psalm 24: 3 - 5
  ^{3} Who may ascend into the hill of the Lord?   And who may stand in His holy place?
  ^{4} He who has clean hands and a pure heart,   Who has not lifted up his soul to falsehood
          And has not sworn deceitfully.
  ^{5} He shall **receive a blessing** from the Lord and righteousness from the God of his salvation.

Now Offer Your Prayer:

Section 3: Jabez Honored God with His Life in spite of His Name

Jabez was trying to honor God with his life even though his name meant "sorrow maker". In a sense he was trying to out run his name to be a blessing to those around him. (I Chronicles 4:9)

Jabez prayed to the God of Israel: "Bless me, O bless me! Give me land, large tracts of land. Provide your personal protection--don't let evil hurt me." God gave him what he asked. (Message)

The Four Major Words - understanding their definitions

  bless - to invoke God , to ask for a blessing . . .
  enlarge - to make large, enlarge, increase . . . even to multiply
  your hand - as in bringing aid, aiding, favoring . . . divine help
  keep me - Creator, produce from yourself, an expression used of living creatures

1 Chronicles 4 : 10 - Jabez cried to the God of Israel, saying,
        "Oh, that You would bless me and enlarge my border, and
          that Your hand might be with me, and You would keep me from evil so it might not
                hurt me! And God granted his request.

Now Offer Your Prayer:

Lesson 1 - Built to Run Together:
Passionate Worship and Zealous Prayer - (page 3)

❖ Why is intermingling praise with prayer and worship with intercession important first to the Lord and second to us?

> Because our prayers and worship rise as Incense before the Lord.
> Then focused prayer riding on top of the zeal of worship becomes an unstoppable force.

❖ What makes a church a house of prayer and worship instead of just a gathering place for friends?
  Why is there joy in the house of prayer?

> The whole community shares the same focus on devotion to Jesus and the importance of using prayer and worship as tools and weapons in His Kingdom.
> Additionally, praying and singing breaks chains and supernatural results follow.

> In His presence is fullness of joy.

❖ Many things happen to and through a person during times of intimate worship and prayer. Name two of the four things listed in this teaching that happen to us when we are a part of deeper worship and passionate prayer.

> Greater Light and Revelation . . . floods into and over us as we invest more time in His presence before the throne of God.

> We are Stronger in Our Ability . . . to get in the flow of intimate worship and prayer because of the extended times of being in His presence.

> Hearts Pure, Minds Focused . . . The power of pure worship used at the highest level is like the Refiners Fire that keeps our hearts pure and our minds focused on the Lord.

> The knowledge of who God is and what He does has become more deeply set in our hearts.

Lesson 2 - Jesus Is The Core of Everything - (page 7)

❖ What are the three things David asked of the Lord in Psalm 27:4? (fill in the blank)

Dwell	**Gaze**	**Inquire**
In the House of the Lord	Upon the beauty	in His Temple

❖ Who is it Heaven sees and how do they respond? Revelation 5: 6, 9 - 10

> **The Person of the Lord Jesus** - Jesus was a real person who walked on the earth. The very being of the Son of God was here in human form and then returned to all of His glory. He is currently seen in Heaven in all of His awesomeness and all of His beauty but now with a glorified body that has scars on it.
>   1. Jesus, the Lamb of God, slain   2. He is beautiful beyond all description
>   3. Heaven sees Him "ever living to make intercession"

❖ What are the three M's and what purpose do they serve?
  On a scale of 1 - 10 with 10 being the highest, how important is humility to Jesus?

> **Model** the truth, **mentor** the ways of the Lord,   and gifts and talents are **multiplied**.

> 10 - Clothe Yourselves with Humility

Lesson 3 - The Prayers of the Saints - Incense Is Rising - (page 10)

❖ As the Elders worshipped the Lamb of God, in Revelation 5, what were they holding in their hands? Why are these elements important to us today?

> Each one holding a harp and golden bowls full of incense
>
> We are Christ's people, covenant-rights people praying in the name of Jesus, by His precious blood. We stand in the power of the life of the crucified Lamb as intercessors.

❖ Why did David love prayer? And why was it important to him?

> Prayer to David denotes both the elevation and enlargement of his desire and the out-goings of his hope and expectation. His prayers rose as incense and an offering.

❖ The power of anointed music through consecrated vessels has its own **authority**.
As anointed music flows, it helps maintain our **concentration** and **focus.**

Lesson 5 - This is Why We Do Corporate Prayer and Worship - (page 17)

❖ What is the ministry Jesus is currently doing and how do we become a part of that?

> He (Jesus) always lives to make intercession.
>
> The fulfilling our priestly calling is to do the ministry of worship and prayer; all believers can be involved in the ministry that Jesus Himself is doing.

❖ In Luke 10:2, there are three major points marked A, B and C. Reread the three points and tell me which one seems the most important to you at this time of your life.

> A. Prayer is Necessary on the Earth because it is Vital for the Harvest
> B. This is What We Know for Sure from Jesus' Words . . .
> C. What We Know for Sure
>   your own personal answer

❖ Name 3 of the 7 aspects of the "Our Father." List them in order of significance to you.

> 1. Jesus declares in this prayer that God is our Father and He reigns from Heaven.
> 2. His name is Holy and as a result, has power to affect change on the earth.
> 3. God's Kingdom is real and it actually exists. Our cry continually then is to be "Your Kingdom come, Your Will be Done." With faith in our hearts we pray it.
> 4. Jesus revealed His own desire and a super important theological point, God desires that what is going on in Heaven would be found on earth in the same way.
> 5. We all have a need for daily bread. So it is our prayer on a daily basis. It is God's desire to give and He made it a part of His promise and provision - daily bread.
> 6. The power to forgive is our choice. No body really wins when we walk in unforgiveness.
> 7. Be aware of the temptations that are around us every day. This is such a great prayer because it ends with deliver us from evil.

Lesson 6 - Psalms, Hymns and Spiritual Songs:
Speak to One Another - (page 21)

❖ It's all about language. I must include the importance of words of encouragement. Ephesians 5 and Colossians 3 tell us almost exactly the same thing. Let the word of Christ richly dwell within you, speak to one another is

Psalms, hymns and spiritual **songs.**

❖ Concerning prophetic worship and prophetic singing, there is a simple definition found in the Hebrew language. The word is naba' - [nä·vä'] which means to sing or speak under the influence of the Divine Spirit. What is the simple five word definition?
(Hint: It's what fountains and gurgling springs do.)

to cause to bubble up

❖ List three of the five categories of Scriptures listed above that are used for Biblical praying.

1. Apostolic prayers of the New Testament –
(Prayers from the heart of God's Apostles and Overseers)
2. Worship Hymns from the Book of Psalms –
(Songs declaring the worth and attributes of the Lord)
3. Prayers from the Book of Psalms –
(Songs of prayer from the Psalmists heart, i.e. David, Asaph)
4. Song of Solomon - The Love Song of the Ravished Heart –
(The story of the interplay between the bride and the bridegroom)
5. Scriptural theophanies - (God revealing Himself to human beings)

Lesson 7 - Because of Love - (page 26)

❖ The reason that we worship is because of Love. The reason that we pray is because of Love. The power to sustain a lifestyle of worship and prayer comes from the

baseline of true love.

❖ Learning the deeper realm of intimacy: 2 Corinthians 13:14 talks about the intimate friendship of the Holy Spirit after mentioning the extravagant love of God.
Write down the importance of intimacy and the realm of friendship as you see or feel it. Recall a time where intimacy or friendship in real life experience made a huge difference in somebody's life.

your own personal answer

❖ Fear is an evil task master. Fear produces lack of confidence, insecurity and nightmares. Perfect love casts out, annihilates and makes fear go away. Why is there no room for fear in love?

Because love produces strength, hope, faith, joy, and an ongoing endurance.
Perfect love **casts out**, annihilates, and makes fear go away.

Lesson 8 - Every Believer's Eternal Identity
Royal Priests unto the Lord - (page 29)

❖ In I Peter 2:9 it clearly states that we are four distinct things as New Testament believers. List them below.

    1. Chosen

    2. Royal Priesthood

    3. Holy Nation

    4. His Own Possession

❖ The powerful person and qualities of the Lord Jesus are displayed in Hebrews 7:2-3.
Most commentators say that when Melchizedek appeared to Abraham in Genesis 14:18 it is the pre-incarnate Christ appearing in the Old Testament. He was establishing the true line of a Holy Priesthood.

What is the meaning of the name Melchizedek? king of righteousness

What three attributes of Melchizedek helped establish the Forever Priesthood?

    1. His name translated means the "king of righteousness," He rules from rightness.

    2. He was referred to as the king of Salem - "king of peace."
       Only Jesus is referred to by these names in both Testaments

    3. This king was without father and without mother and even without genealogy.
       No natural man could claim this category.

❖ It is a great honor to be a part of fulfilling the Priestly Ministry of worship and intercession. Our spiritual offerings are simply our **Music**, our **Worship** and our **Prayers**.

Lesson 9 - Intercession: The Power to Intervene - (page 33)

❖ Give an example of how you have had to stand up for justice and against injustice in your life.

    your own personal answer

❖ How can we use our tongue for the power of blessing? (example: encouragement, compliments, etc.) List out the forms of speaking and words that do not bring a blessing.

    your own personal answer

❖ Our Test: keep track for one day, the five most positive / negative things that you say out loud.

    your own personal answer

Lesson 11 - Flowing in New Songs and Songs of the Holy Spirit
(Page 38)

❖ Breaking out into spiritual songs is one of the coolest forms of singing.
Ephesians 5:19 says this "but drink **deeply** of God's Spirit. **Speak** out to one another in psalms, hymns and spiritual songs **joining** with one another in holy **songs** of praise and of the Spirit."

❖ Why are spiritual songs important in the Prayer Room?

The use of spiritual songs in the Prayer Room is one of our greatest foundational tools. It allows singers and musicians to adlib, flowing in the river of God. They can create songs of the moment with lyrics full of the Word of God.

❖ Name three ways can we fulfill Acts 13:22 in our own lives, becoming like David who was called a man after God's own heart.

1. your own personal answers

2.

3.

Lesson 12 - If My People, Called by My Name, Humble Themselves
(Page 41)

❖ In 2 Chronicles 7: 12 -16 in your opinion list the top three elements of the nine listed within that Scripture and include a simple explanation of "why."

your own personal answers

❖ What are the reasons that people don't engage in becoming devoted worshippers or dedicated intercessors?

your own personal answers

❖ God gave us a promise that He will hear from Heaven, forgive our sins and heal our land. In 2 Chronicles 7:14. To you, which is the greatest miracle out of these three things that God has promised and offered to do?

I realize that this is really a difficult question but it is so good for us to think and process through it.

your own personal answers

Lesson 13 - The Weapons of Our Spiritual Warfare are Mighty
(Page 46)

❖ On a scale of 1 - 10 (ten being the highest), how important is it that people see that every believer is called to high level prayer and worship, to actually function as prayer warriors?

your own personal answers

❖ For though we walk in the **flesh**, we do not **war** according to the flesh.

Human indeed we are, but it is in no **human strength** that we fight our battles.

. . . for the weapons of our warfare (**arms** of our **knighthood**) are not of the flesh but are divinely powerful.

❖ Through the power of the anointing of God's presence, singing, worshipping and playing music unto the Lord becomes an unstoppable force.'
Review 2 Chronicles 20: 18 - 25. List out the top 3 most important points from this passage and write out a paragraph on each point.

your own personal answers

Lesson 14 - Singing and Praying the Word of God - (Page 50)

❖ There is a great need for people to know the Bible. They need to have the Word of God deeply planted in the hearts. The book of Romans records that faith comes by hearing and hearing by the Word of God. How would you implement the singing and memorization of the Word of God for your life, your church and your friends?

your own personal answers

❖ Let the teaching of Christ and His words keep on **living** in you. Keep on teaching and helping each other. Sing the Songs of **David** and the church songs and the songs of **Heaven** with hearts full of thanks to God.

❖ Concerning holy songs of praise and songs of the Spirit: why is it important that singers and musicians understand these two realms?

These two categories give us the freedom to venture out to sing more from our hearts than from our minds. It's found and accessed much more in the presence based orientation. The anchor point is the same for all of us.

Lesson 15 - The High Praises of God and Two Edged Sword - (Page 54)

❖ How wonderful is it to know that the high praises of God in your mouth and the Word of God coming from your heart has the power of Heaven standing behind it? Explain why your words and melodies are important both to the Lord and in this world.

❖ From Psalm 37:28 - 30 "For the **Lord** loves **justice** and does not forsake His godly one. The mouth of the **righteous** utters wisdom and his **tongue** speaks justice.

❖ With Jesus, real authority comes from three distinct realms.
      One: Who He is as the **King** of **Glory**.
      Two: What He has done as the **Crucified Lamb** of God.
      Three: His place in Heaven and His return as the **Victorious Lion**

Lesson 16 - Urgency! Take Heed, Watch and Pray - (Page 58)

❖ TAKE HEED defined in military and police terms goes like this, "your head should be on a swivel." It is referring to walking around with **360** degree vision and sensitivity. So how would you change your lifestyle to be more on guard and sensitive the Spirit and peoples needs around you?

> your own personal answers

❖ WATCH: The element of "watching" opens the door for us to what?

> **Move into a greater awakening**

Because our prayers, worship and intercession affect change in what two dimensions?

> **time and the spirit dimension**

❖ PRAY: Review the four prayer principles found in Mark 13 and write down which one is most important to you and why?

> **First** truth - Prayer brings light and illumination.

> **Second** truth - Do not be troubled, only have a pray-full spirit.

> **Third** truth - Take heed, watch and pray.

> **Fourth** truth - Jesus' counsel in light of it all, "I say to all: Watch!"

Lesson 17 - God Trains Our Hands for War, Our Fingers for Battle
(Page 61)

❖ Why would there be a need for the Lord to train our hands for war and our fingers for battle?

> **...so that my arms can bend a bow of bronze...**

> **God must train us so that we can be strong and defeat our enemies.**

Don't overlook the obvious in answering this question. All of us have **enemies**.

❖ If you had a choice to be a "worshipping warrior" or a "warring worshipper," which would you choose and why?

(Remember the adjective comes first, because it describes the noun.
But the noun declares the subject. So when the describer goes away, what are you?)

> your own personal answers

❖ According to Colossians 2, Jesus has **disarmed** the **rulers** and **authorities**.

He made a bold public display of them, having **triumphed** over them.

He **spoiled** the principalities and powers that were ranged against us.

Lesson 18 - Anointed Prayer and Worship Release God's Justice

❖ We are the servants of the Lord who stand as prophetic worshipping **intercessors**.

As we pray, we release the stored up, transforming power of His Word. We have the **honor**, as friends of the **Bridegroom**, to help establish His Kingdom's coming and seeing thousands turn to the Lord as the **darkness** comes off of them.

❖ Why is it important that we pray the Word concerning justice and judgment?
Think of this question in light of Psalm 37's declarations:

(a) "the Lord loves justice and   (b) the tongue of the righteous speaks justice."

your own personal answers

❖ We have powerful resources and weapons in the Lord. Ephesians 6:11

*Put on God's whole armor [the armor of **a heavy-armed soldier** which God supplies], that you may be able successfully to stand up against [all] the strategies and the deceits of the devil.*

List the two most important and powerful elements in this verse.

1. _____

2. _____

Made in the USA
San Bernardino, CA
03 August 2014